A Child Shall Lead

*How God Walks You Through Darkness
with Hope, Wisdom and Healing*

By Carla Anne Hart

elevate faith

Advanced Praise for *A Child Shall Lead*

Here are the seasoned reflections of one who has learned to see all of life—even our most desperate and dire circumstances—through the eyes of faith. Carla Hart has much to teach us about "becoming as children" as Jesus said, that we might see Him walking in the midst of every challenge we face. If you're looking for an anecdote to the cynicism and irony that plagues this generation, you've found it in *A Child Shall Lead*.

Carey Cash, Author,
A Table in the Presence: The Dramatic Account of How a U.S. Marine Battalion Experienced God's Presence Amidst the Chaos of the War in Iraq

Eighteen years ago, my life was irretrievably altered when I was called to the bedside of a dying child who summoned me, asking if her 'life had made a difference.' In *A Child Shall Lead*, Carla Hart explores 20 years of experiences that likewise altered her worldview with exceptional clarity, compassion and understanding, all informed by a vigorous faith. Ms. Hart has an uncommon ability to see the gifts that every one brings to the world—even in seemingly untenable situations—and shares her insights to our benefit. Ms. Hart challenges all to 'take a look' and I would urge you to join this extraordinary journey. Your life could be changed!

David Phillips, Ed.D.
Lankenau Medical Center

Carla is able to capture the "essence" of the spirit of the children, families, staff, and people she has encountered on her life journey. The book illustrates the human spirit and she is able to eloquently express what God has done in her life through her interactions with others. As a child life specialist, I had the opportunity to see her "works in action" and through her writings, she is able to paint a vivid portrait for all to see of her experiences working with pediatric patients.

Renee Hunte, MA, CCLS

We are all put on this earth to travel a journey. There are happy times, bumps and bruises along the way, and sometimes, indescribable heartache. The one truth is that God understands...and knowingly puts the right people in our path to walk our journey with us. Carla Hart IS a blessing that God had chosen. The way she has touched so many lives is a testament to the beautiful soul that lives within her. Reading this book will restore your faith in humanity. We all have the ability to change someone's life...Carla already has.

Patti Deppe
Mom of Sarah Grace

Advanced Praise

In every profession you will find those who are, quite simply, passionate about what they do. I have encountered them in all types of positions and all walks of life. They love what they do and they end up making a difference in the lives of others while having their own lives enriched beyond their wildest dreams. It is who they are, and they really don't know what else they would do in life besides what they are doing. In thirty-three years of ministering to hospitalized children and their families, in hospitals and camps throughout the United States, I have met no one more passionate about her work than Carla. I am honored to know her as a friend and so glad that she has opened up her journey to the rest of us in the pages of this book.

Woody Wolfe
Director, Heart to Hand Ministries, Inc.

A Child Shall Lead is an inspirational and compelling look at the lives of some very small people who are facing very big problems. Carla has given us a view into their world, with compassionate storytelling and spiritual wisdom. These accounts give us a reason for hope beyond hope, and help us to see light even in the darkest places.

Mark Traylor
Pastor, Eastwind Community Church

A Child Shall Lead

It was achingly wonderful to read this book! Having recently gone through cancer treatment with our 10-year-old son, I read, with tears streaming down my face, these heartrending stories of resilience, courage, suffering, revelation .The Biblical quotes ground the experiences described and put spiritual context in the most human of circumstances. I highly recommend this book to all people who have gone through or are going through situations for which there is no roadmap. It speaks to the beauty and enrichment that can be found in the most difficult experiences. Having been repeatedly humbled and inspired by my child, these messages spoke to me uniquely. Carla walked with us though our son's treatment with the education and neurocognitive consequences of his brain surgery, chemotherapy and radiation. With this book she once again lovingly inspired, encouraged and supported us as we continue to love a child and family who went through the unimaginable. Please take the time to read this wonderful book!

Mary Dittrich, MD, FASN

Advanced Praise

Life does not always make sense. When our livelihood is threatened unexpectedly, we suddenly realize how fragile, complex, and vulnerable we are.

A Child Shall Lead is a beautiful collage of true stories about people confronted with life-altering circumstances who must overcome seemingly insurmountable odds, fear, and doubt. Carla Hart takes us on a journey into the deepest part of the human experience where life and death hangs in the balance, and where grace and love are abundant.

This book gently touches our emotions, inspiring faith and courage to beat the odds. Written from an eyewitness account, Carla shows us how God often uses the most unlikely encounters with people to demonstrate His compassion and bring about healing. These stories reveal our need to live in right relationship with God and each other. In this way we find lasting peace and joy, even in the midst of pain and suffering.

Kevin Mark
Executive Director, Wind & Wheat Ministries

Copyright © 2014 by Carla Anne Hart

Editorial Work by AnnaMarie McHargue
Cover Design by Bobby Kuber
Interior Layout by Leslie Hertling

All rights reserved. No portion of this book may be reproduced, stored in a retrieval system, or transmitted in any form or by any means © electronic, mechanical, photocopy, recording, scanning, or other © except for brief quotations in critical reviews or articles, without the prior written permission of the publisher.

Scripture quotations marked NIV are taken from the *Holy Bible, New International Version*.® niv®. Copyright © 1973, 1978, 1984, by International Bible Society.

Published in Boise, Idaho by Elevate Faith, a division of Elevate Publishing.
www.elevatepub.com

For information please email: info@elevatepub.com.

ISBN (print): 978-1937498573
Printed in the United States of America

Table of Contents

Introduction	1
Second Chances	5
Hurricane	13
Strength	27
Acceptance	33
Bullies	47
Joy	53
Hope	59
Peace	81
Fluff	91
Slurpees and Other Simple Acts of Kindness	97
Judgment	105
Irony of It All	113
Sincerity	125
Slow Motion	133
Wailing Wall	141
My Story	147
In Closing: Discovery	157
Acknowledgments	160

Dedication

To my angels, my messengers—those seen and unseen who have inspired and led me along this journey.

Introduction

"Blessed are the poor in spirit, for theirs is the kingdom of heaven. Blessed are those who mourn, for they will be comforted."
Matthew 5:3-4

I work in a place many people call "Hope." Maybe people call it that while they are there because hope is the only thing they have to hold on to. Hope is a powerful tool. It provides strength. It is positive. Hope brings people together.

These are the things I know to be true.

Every day, people who work to heal others in need surround me. I watch chaplains bow their heads and whisper words of prayer. I see social workers sitting with families who struggle to make sense of their upside-down world. I walk past therapists in the hallway as they coach patients to move forward one foot at a time.

Nurses hustle from room to room checking their patients' vitals and medications. Doctors stand at the bedside relaying information that may or may not provide comfort to those listening.

Child life specialists provide distraction to ease the fear in a screaming child. Teachers listen as their students share what it feels like to be questioned and teased about things they have no way to control.

Everyone is absorbing the emotions that surround us. Much of the time we are unaware of how this impacts our own life.

I see it in their eyes as they stare blankly ahead while eating their lunch in the break room. I hear it in their voices as they crack during brief conversations. Body postures reveal fatigue. Tears sometimes stream down cheeks without warning.

These healers are my friends. They have dedicated their lives to helping people when they are in greatest need. But with that gift comes sacrifice. The memories of the day scar the healers and can bring pain that may last a lifetime.

Each day in the hospital brings a new circumstance. Experiences come in different ways. Some are more difficult than others. Some are sheer fun.

All are a gift if you open yourself up to the messages that are being offered to you while you travel through the emotion.

I've watched my friends suffer silently, often unaware that the weight of their work is accumulating on their souls. I want to help them heal, too. I want to show them the gift, the "Light" that shines in each of these unique situations.

I have been graced with the ability to see these gifts clearly. People like to tell me that they couldn't do what I do. That it would be too hard, too sad or too depressing.

Introduction

Some people say they "are too sensitive," and therefore they could never work in a hospital doing what I do. I just smile, shake my head and smile some more. What does that mean? Does it mean that I am heartless and without emotion?

Actually, what it means is that I notice resilience, tenacity, renewal, love, gentleness, survival and hope. What I do and what I witness is hard; at times, it is sad and certainly can get frustrating and depressing, but most of the time, it is so much more.

The "more" is the part that keeps me going back every day. The "more" is that part that I want to share. It makes my encounters, what I experience and what I do make sense in this hectic, full-speed-ahead world of ours. But it doesn't always come easily.

There have been days when I've wanted to quit and go work in a coffee shop where it's latte or cappuccino, not life or death. I've questioned my purpose and my impact, wondering if I actually am making a positive difference in this world.

The answers to these questions are presented before me every day. I remind myself to look up, open my eyes and actually see what has been laid before me as my answer. This is a difficult task, to unveil healing in the midst of such discord.

Immediate action is needed knowing this difficult task. I cannot do this alone. Someone must make room for this "Light" and speak for Jesus, as He controls all things.

Who will perform this great duty? It will take someone who is *"blessed."* Someone who can see clearly the value found within the gifts. Someone who can share the experience of hope and joy, independent of outward circumstances. Someone who can serve as an instrument for our healing.

Turn your head and take a look.

"Here I am! He sent me..."

And a little *child* shall lead.

Chapter One
Second Chances

❋   ❋   ❋

> *"Do not conform any longer to the pattern of the world, but be transformed by the renewing of your mind. Then you will be able to test and approve what God's will is—His good, pleasing and perfect will."*
> Romans 12:2

Meet my friend Rosario, a 15-year-old with a football-sized tumor in his stomach.

A nurse, probably out of desperation, asked me to meet with him. "We have a teenager here who will be here for an unspecified amount of time, and we don't know what to do with him... we need a teacher! *STAT!*"

Rosario told me later that people judged him (telling him to his face or deciding for themselves) what type of person he was based on how he looked.

Rosario had long, dark, waist-length hair. It was thick, wavy and gorgeous! He pierced his eyebrow and his ears and sported at least one tattoo. He told me that other than his mom, everyone around him rejected him. It didn't matter what he said or how he said it, Rosario was called a loser and told he'd never become anything good.

Rosario had a tough exterior and understandably protected himself with an armor of defensiveness. His heart was hurting, but that was something he planned to keep to himself.

I walked into his room to introduce myself and was greeted angrily with, "I'm not in school. I *HATE* school! You are wasting your time with me."

Awesome! I love a challenge.

I told him a little bit about how "school" worked with me and how school worked in our hospital. I shared that I expected all students to come one time and try it. If they "hated" it and never wanted to come back after that one experience, then I would respect their wishes.

What I didn't tell him was that I've never had a student who didn't return. Everyone comes back.

Rosario looked at me for a long moment, I'm sure contemplating if what I said was indeed fact. I stared back into his eyes and smiled, then I said, "I've got all day for you, I'm going to sit here until you decide to come with me."

He looked flustered and started pacing in his room. Finally, he said, "O.K., fine, but I have to brush my teeth first."

Unbeknownst to him, that was the first day of his transformation.

It began with a choice, a risk and a chance for himself. He bet on himself one more time, maybe in his heart, "one last time." He chose "YES" and that's all we needed.

As we walked down to the classroom, I wondered what it might take to captivate Rosario's mind into wanting to come back tomorrow. God's grace was present, and His ideas and creativity were everywhere when we had our session.

After learning that he used to like English class, I decided to take a risk on Shakespeare. *Romeo and Juliet.* I know. Groan. Would this actually keep him coming back for more? I thought it might. In fact, I believed this story would resonate with Rosario on many realms, and I was right.

Rosario came back the next day and the next, eager to learn more each time.

We explored the history of the time period, the art, the background of Shakespeare and how he came to write that story, all the while intertwining Rosario's life experiences and passions into the lessons of the day.

I loved hearing Rosario's Hispanic accent articulate the words of Shakespeare, his pronunciations bringing a new twist to the old tale.

What started happening next was nothing less than amazing.

One day, as I approached his hospital room, I noticed a group of his friends inside. I thought to myself, *O.K., he is going to try to get out of school to hang out with his friends.*

Rosario introduced me to each friend, also telling me a little of their story. I could tell that each seemed nervous around me. Some of the young men had been in jail for various reasons. None of them had finished high school; all had dropped out or been kicked out.

I looked from face to face wondering why they looked so nervous. So, I turned and asked Rosario, "Are you ready for school today?" He said, "Yes, but I wanted to know if my friends could come, too?"

I stared in excited disbelief. "You guys want to come to school, too?" I asked. They stammered out, "Yeah, are we allowed?"

"Sure," I said, "We're studying *Romeo and Juliet*, and we need more characters. Are you guys up for learning Shakespeare and taking a part?" In unison, they chanted, "Yes!"

These boys walked into a *children's* hospital to learn. They were far from being children. They wanted a second chance.

I grew to love these boys and wanted to see them in school everyday. I knew if we had time, their lives could change for the better.

That is one of the difficult parts about my job. You don't wish any of these kids would be in the hospital; however, there are times when being in the hospital is a positive catalyst for their life.

Sometimes, I wonder whom it benefits more, them or me? They teach me so much. I learn about life, love, hardships, courage, dedication and faith. I learn everyday and I am so thankful for those opportunities.

Most of the days in the hospital, I did not see Rosario's mom. On occasion she would be in the room when I went to pick him up for class, and I would say *hello* and let her know what we had done to date in school. I also shared the plans for that day.

She always stared at me with a look that was hard for me to decipher. I didn't know if she was mad, uninterested or something else.

Chapter One: Second Chances

About two months into Rosario's hospitalization, I entered the elevator at the lobby level. In walked Rosario's mom as well. After my *hello*, we rode up to the pediatric floor in silence. Again, I didn't quite know how to interpret her actions.

As we walked off the elevator toward the patient rooms she turned to me suddenly and said in a gruff voice, "I don't know what you are doing to my son!"

Her body had turned so that my back was against the wall and she was standing close to me—you know, in that invisible space that can make it uncomfortable if someone you don't want in there steps inside.

I said in the calmest voice that I could muster, "I am not sure what you mean. Do you have a question about what we are doing in school?"

She said, "Yes, I can't believe what you've done!" Again sounding as though there was a problem.

I had to have looked confused as she continued her thought. She went on to explain her home was smack in the middle of gang territory. She never wanted her kids to be in a gang.

She had high expectations for all of her kids, and she wanted them to succeed and complete high school so they could get out of that neighborhood for good.

She admitted that people looked at them and made judgments about the kind of people they were, and that the teachers in the schools had done the same thing to her and were now doing it to her children. She saw her own kids and their friends drop out of school, one by one giving up, as there seemed to be no one who had enough faith in them to help them through.

She wanted better for her son, and now here he was in the hospital.

Tears welled in her eyes as her demeanor changed. Her posture softened and she continued, "I don't know what you're doing with my son, but I thank you. He is different than he was before we came here. I can see the son I had hoped he could become and it is because of you and what you are teaching him here. I may not understand the books and the work, but I do know what is good and this, what he is getting here, is good."

She thanked me for believing in him and in her. She thanked me for not judging them by the way they lived or the way they looked.

She turned and walked away.

I was left standing there for a minute processing what had just happened. Hallway drive-bys. That's what I call those moments. This drive-by was good. Really, really good.

As his body healed, so did his spirit. After several months my time in school with Rosario ended. It was a happy and sad day for us both. He had accomplished so much and he was excited about learning again. We said our goodbyes knowing that this moment might be our last together.

I couldn't help but wonder if he would continue on with schooling or if his neighborhood would extinguish his flame.

It was about a month later when Rosario came back to pay me a visit. He was at the hospital for a follow-up appointment with his surgeon.

Chapter One: Second Chances

He looked amazing! His coloring was great. His hair was still long, thick and beautiful, and he had braided it neatly down his back. His piercings were out. And best of all, his guard was down.

He emitted peace.

While we were catching up on the month that had passed, he brought out a picture of his new girlfriend. He beamed as he talked about how they had met and who she was as a person. He also let me know that he had re-enrolled in high school and was on track to graduate.

He looked and sounded so happy. He thanked me for helping him and said he felt "lucky" that he had developed that tumor in his gut. He said his life would not have changed for the better without having been put in our hospital.

His relationship with his mom and sisters was stronger and the love he had for himself had been restored.

As he walked away, he turned with a smile and asked me one last question: "Miss Carla, if I ever have to come back to the hospital for a long period of time again, can we read *Hamlet*?"

Now that's a good day!

My prayer for you:

❋ ❋ ❋

DO NOT CONFORM ANY LONGER TO THE PATTERN OF THE WORLD, BUT BE TRANSFORMED BY THE RENEWING OF YOUR MIND. THEN YOU WILL BE ABLE TO TEST AND APPROVE WHAT GOD'S WILL IS—HIS GOOD, PLEASING AND PERFECT WILL.

IT IS HURTFUL WHEN PEOPLE JUDGE US WITHOUT KNOWING OUR LIVES, CIRCUMSTANCES OR WHAT WE HAVE ENDURED. AT TIMES, WE ARE GUILTY OF THIS ACT OURSELVES, INFLICTING JUDGMENT ONTO OTHERS WITHOUT UNDERSTANDING THEIR COMPREHENSIVE SITUATION, OR THEIR STORY.

GOD, I ASK THAT YOU BLOCK THESE HURTFUL AND JUDGING THOUGHTS FROM ENTERING OUR HEARTS, OUR MINDS. I ASK THAT YOU FILL US INSTEAD WITH GRACE, WITH COMPASSION AND GENTLENESS SO THAT WE CAN BE A SOURCE OF LIGHT TO THOSE WHO ARE AROUND US.

THIS I ASK IN YOUR NAME. AMEN.

Chapter Two
Hurricane

❃   ❃   ❃

"For it is by grace you have been saved, through faith—and this not from yourselves, it is the gift of God—not by works, so that no one can boast. For we are God's workmanship, created in Christ Jesus to do good works, which God prepared in advance for us to do." Ephesians 2: 8-10

I might die.
This thought briefly crossed my mind as I raced home from work to pack a few belongings, trying to outrun an incoming hurricane.

The only family I had near me was my chocolate lab, Bean. Everyone else lived in states far away. I wasn't even sure if they were aware of what was happening along the coast. I didn't have time to call; I needed to get on the road.

The sky was turning dark and I was becoming anxious.

I have lived in many places but have never been in a hurricane. What was I suppose to do? It was just my dog and me, and I was scared.

Come on, think! I said to myself. *What do you actually need to survive?* I quickly made a mental list of items that I would use if we got stranded on the road. Flashlights, batteries, water, packaged food items, dog food, blanket, first aid kit, phone, phone charger, tape...what else?

Next, I thought about items that I might need later, should my house be destroyed in the storm. I ran upstairs and grabbed files with my Social Security card, insurance papers, birth certificate, and several family photos. I threw in a few nostalgic items for memory's sake and began packing my car.

My car wasn't big. It was old and on its last legs, but it had four working wheels and was full of gas, so I loaded it up. I prayed it would keep us safe during our journey.

Once the car was packed, I remembered I thought about moving my furniture upstairs to the highest point in the house so that if flooding occurred, I could save as much as possible. I guess I was lucky that I didn't have any living room furniture at the time. My bedroom was on the first floor and there was no way that I could lift the bed and my dresser by myself, so I shrugged that off and walked away.

I grabbed a sleeping bag and some camping stuff and thought that at least I could camp if I didn't have a house.

My heart was beating quickly. It was an eerie feeling knowing that something huge and completely out of my control was about to happen. I didn't know when or even where I was going to be when this act of God occurred.

After the last hurricane, people shared stories of running out of gas on the highway, discovering out-of-town hotels

Chapter Two: Hurricane

that were too full to take more guests and waiting for weeks for help to arrive.

During the last sweep of my house, I spotted one unopened bottle of wine sitting on my counter. I grabbed it along with an opener and two plastic glasses thinking, *What the heck, if I get stranded on the highway I might as well make a friend and share some wine.* Coping.

I got into the car with my lab and started slowly driving away. I looked for my neighbors but couldn't find any of them. The streets looked abandoned. I didn't get to say goodbye. What if I never saw them again? They were my friends and I cared about what happened to them. I wanted to say goodbye. Without warning, my body starting shaking.

Deep breaths. Focus. Silent prayers filled my head asking for safety for my friends and myself, guidance, peace and knowledge to endure whatever lay ahead. I headed toward the highway in the direction of a neighborhood north of the city. The storm was slated to hit in the southern region where I lived and the news was promising that neighborhoods up north were safe. I was going to be staying with a couple and their children whom I had met one month before when they moved to town. Strangers in essence, but we were all we had.

When I arrived at their home, the children greeted me first. They were excited for my "visit" and couldn't wait to show me around. Their mom and I went along holding their hands while they bounced around showing me their rooms, their backyard and their games. "What are we going to do first?" they squealed. They were so excited, completely unaware of what was about to happen. They were innocently living in the moment, trusting and without fear.

Their mom stared at me with trepidation in her eyes. I quickly realized that I was the one who the family looked upon as the "leader." They needed me to set the tone for how this was going to play out.

I decided then and there that we all would make this into an "adventure," with the thrill of the unexpected looming around us. Because we were new to this area, we didn't have pre-made boards for the windows stored in our garages. We were dependent on tape so that if the windows shattered, the glass would at least be contained.

We told the kids we needed to get some items for the big indoor camping trip we all were about to take. They were giddy as we drove to the closest store to stock up on water, dry food, propane, batteries and tape. People were everywhere and the shelves were almost bare. We managed to get one case of water and a few snack crackers. Propane, batteries and tape were nowhere to be found.

At home, I set the "expectations" for our campout. I asked the kids to make a play area in the crawl space underneath the stairs. This was one of the only rooms in the house that was windowless. They ran around gathering blankets and toys, setting them up for play. While they were busy doing that, the adults prepared flashlights, batteries and chargers for the phones. We filled the bathtubs with water in the case that we'd need it in the days to come.

We watched the news, which showed terrifying pictures of the quickly approaching force. The wind began to howl,

Chapter Two: Hurricane

shaking the windows and whistling around the doors. The noise was nothing like I've ever heard.

Luckily, I had brought what tape I had at home, and we started taping the windows on the first floor.

Our anxiety increased as we saw lawn furniture and umbrellas flying across the neighbors' yard. Thoughts whirled around my head. I was terrified; I didn't know what we were doing. It was like the blind leading the blind, yet I needed to keep it together so that we all wouldn't fall apart.

God was present every step of the way. He *had* to be. I knew this because as soon as a terrifying thought would enter my brain, it was replaced with peace. Instantly. Each time.

The hours passed and then it grew dark. We lost electricity and all was still. *What is this? What's going to happen next?* We all sat in the living room, mindlessly playing games with the kids. Bean was there, too, calm and without concern. I used him as my gauge. Animals have a keen sense of what is happening around them and I thought, *as long as he is calm, I'll be calm, too.* I figured he'd let me know when all mayhem was about to break lose.

The storm wasn't supposed to reach the neighborhood where we were. That was the theory at least. Reality was that it had moved, and we were centered directly beneath the force of the storm.

Even though our phones had been charged, we were unable to send or receive any messages. We couldn't contact anyone, and we didn't know if anyone had tried to contact us. Did our friends and relatives even know what was happening?

After two full days, it became clear that we had no timeline for the duration of what we'd endure. We set a schedule for opening the refrigerator and planned what we would take out during our rationed time. We ate the food that would spoil first, along with the milk, saving the packaged items for last.

The wind was so strong it sent the rain into the house through the air vents and windows. It literally was raining sideways, inside the house. We kept towels rolled along the doors and windows, hoping this was all we would need to keep the house dry.

It was hard to decipher day from night, as there was no sense of time. The noises were unbearable. Wind vibrated against tree limbs as they banged into windows. Doors shook as if they were about to explode. Windows bowed in and out, withstanding forces that at any moment could send them shattering. The noise didn't stop for three full days.

For safety, we all slept in the walk-in closet on the first floor. Each night, I prayed diligently for safety for all of us, for clarity and for peace. Amazingly, the kids and Bean acted as if none of this was fazing them. They were on an adventure, after all, and it was fun! It was as if my prayers were being answered before I even asked.

On the third day of the storm, all became still. The rain and wind had stopped and the sky was a yellowish orange with shadows of black all around. I had never seen anything like it. There were no birds, no squirrels, no wind, no sounds. The silence was disturbing and surreal.

Chapter Two: Hurricane

People started peeking outside and walking around their driveways, not wanting to go too far. We brought camping chairs onto the porch. Neighbors gathered and we decided to grill the meat we were going to lose from the freezers. We kept close, none of us knowing when the wind and rain might start up again.

Kids ran and giggled, playing as if nothing was going on. I felt a sense of freedom from the days of being trapped inside. Bean never left my side. He was my calming force, gently walking beside me offering wordless reassurance.

What we didn't know at the time was that we were in the "eye" of the storm. For those of you who don't know what that means, it's the calm part of the storm before the worst part happens. The back end of a hurricane can bring even more force than the beginning. Sometimes, it is a blessing to be unaware.

After the cookout, we all separated and went back into our shelters. It was another three days of storm before the rain and wind stopped again. This time, things looked different. The sky was gray and white and there was a slight breeze blowing. Inside, we heard beeps emerging from one of our phones; there were messages waiting for us.

Relief washed over me as I heard voices from friends, family and the neighbors I had been so worried about. I knew where they were and that they were O.K., but they didn't know where I was. They were worried. I wanted so badly to contact them, but my phone wouldn't allow me to make calls.

We walked outside to see if any of the neighbors had service. Most were like us, receiving stored messages but un-

A Child Shall Lead

able to send any out. One neighbor had a generator that powered a radio. He was able to tell us that the storm had passed and we were in the clear. We survived. *Thank God!* We still had no power but we were still alive. There were so many emotions and thoughts running through my mind. I just wanted to settle down so I could focus on returning to my home across the city.

We organized the "camping" site and I repacked my car with my belongings. I took some of the water, a few rations of food and my flashlight, phone and half of the batteries. None of us knew how long it would be until power was restored. I said goodbye to the kids and to my new friends. We started as strangers and grew to be family.

Leaving was terrifying. I wanted to stay in the secure nest we had built, yet I needed to find out if my own house still stood. I drove away, looking back only once to see my "family" standing on their porch, waving goodbye.

As I approached the highway, I was met with absolute desolation. Signposts were gone, lights vanished, storefronts demolished. Trees and branches were everywhere, twisted and piled in all directions. All I could see was a lone procession of cars inching slowly in cadence down a vast open road.

Tears welled in my eyes and I started to sob uncontrollably. *What if I can't make it home?* I made it through the storm surrounded by God's presence, peace and friends. But now I felt more alone than I'd ever felt in my life.

I actually stopped my car, right there on the highway. There was no one behind me and I didn't care. I stopped, grabbing the steering wheel while I lowered my head, rest-

Chapter Two: Hurricane

ing it on my hands. I prayed again for peace, for safety and for guidance.

Again, I felt it immediately. This time, however, was different. It was almost as if I could see and feel Jesus sitting in the passenger seat beside me. He was smiling, reassuring me that I wasn't alone and that He would be with me the whole way home.

What should have been a 45-minute drive home took me almost three hours to complete. I have no idea how I had enough gas to make it, but I wasn't worried. I knew I was being protected.

As I rounded the corner to my street I saw it: my house, still standing. I didn't see much damage. It, too, had survived the storm.

There is nothing like an act of God (natural disaster) to show us the meaning behind living, sharing, compassion, grace, joy, gratefulness, His power, His protection and His love.

I witnessed this firsthand and in the months to come would be able to testify more confidently to His awesomeness.

The devastation of this hurricane lasted for over a year. Some neighborhoods were without power for several months and didn't receive help for weeks. This was not covered on the news, so most people were unaware that the suffering continued.

One day, in the midst of all the pain around me, I received a phone call from my uncle, who lived in another state. He said he was coming to help with the storm cleanup and asked if I was interested in helping him. "Sure!" I said.

I had no idea how that answer would change my life.

After he arrived, he told me that the first thing we were going to do was sort food. Seemed easy enough. I can sort food. We drove out into the countryside to an establishment that looked like a cross between a warehouse and farm. We entered a house and met several people. They worked there and were telling us about the shipments (of food) that had just arrived. Around back were trucks filled with crates of food from grocery stores, and it was that that we were to sort.

I also noticed a group of volunteers wearing matching t-shirts that advertised the name of their church. I had actually attended service there a few times, so I went over to introduce myself. I was taken aback when I was met with condescension. I walked away confused but focused on the task ahead.

We were all assigned different crates to sort through. The "volunteers" picked the easy foods like soda and chip bags to sort, as those only required looking for an expiration date. I was left with vegetation, sorting through perishables for anything still edible. It was messy and sometimes smelly, but I didn't mind. After all, I had survived a hurricane with my house intact, power re-established and Jesus at my side. I was grateful for my blessings.

Why didn't these others feel and behave the same? I observed as they kept checking their watches as though they were only present to fulfill a requirement. I guess they didn't understand that it is not our "good deeds" that will get us to Heaven, but our relationship with God Himself. God knows what's in our hearts, and "putting in time"

Chapter Two: Hurricane

doing something that isn't in your heart to do is a waste. Their behavior made me angry, as I didn't want them to be the example for others who were searching for a relationship with Christ.

The day continued until dark when my uncle told me it was time to stop. Tomorrow we would be back at it.

The next morning we were asked to load up three trucks with the food and drinks and drive them into the neighborhoods that had the most need. Only one truck showed up. It was old and barely ran. It was all we had, so the loading process began.

My uncle and I got into the truck. As I turned to grab the seatbelt I noticed that where it once hung sat just the hook. We looked at each other and joked about being pulled over by the police. It wouldn't be for speeding, actually the opposite as the truck only managed 40 miles per hour. We were off.

As we were approaching the neighborhood, my uncle asked me if I was ready. "Ready for what?" I asked naively. He explained that he'd never been in this particular neighborhood, heard it was a little rough and didn't really know what we'd encounter. He reminded me that these people had been without power and food for at least a month, some maybe longer. He didn't know what their frame of mind would be.

For a moment, I was afraid as I sensed his trepidation. As soon as that feeling came, it disappeared and once again I was calm.

We rounded the corner and there they were. Lined up for blocks, waiting. There were so many people. Young, old, able-bodied, weak. *Will we have enough food for them all,* I wondered.

As we got closer, I observed that there was order amongst them. Each person stood in line casually; talking to one another like it was an ordinary day. Some held a box or bag, while others held laundry baskets. They each held a tiny piece of paper as well. "What's on the paper?" I whispered to my uncle. "Numbers," he said. "Each piece of paper has a number on it and that's how they know what order to stand in. That's the order in which they'll receive their food."

I stared at him in disbelief. Who decided that, and how did they know the people would obey? Not only were they following the rules, they were smiling and talking to one another. The children were playing in the street, not concerned in the least that they might not be fed.

As we pulled into the church parking lot, a pastor and some of his volunteers greeted us. The difference between this group and the volunteers the day before was radical. There was no anger, no greed, no pushing or rushing. It was if they were all there attending a summer picnic with friends.

As my uncle talked to the pastor about the system for handing out the food, I opened the back of the truck to begin the unloading process. I stood in the truck cavity and turned with a box in my hand to see dozens of eager faces staring up at me. Their hands were outstretched, not wanting to grab the food, rather to offer me help in carrying the load.

Several men said, "You can get down from there, ma'am, we will do the work." At first I declined, stating, "It's O.K.,

Chapter Two: Hurricane

I want to help." Time stopped for a moment, their faces captured in a frame. What I saw and heard next was astonishing.

"Please ma'am, we need to do this for ourselves. We are so thankful for this food and for your time to bring it to us. You'll never know what this means to us. We can't do much, but we can help each other in times of need, and by letting us sort this food for our neighbors, we feel like we are contributing."

These people were united as one, proud to be able to offer help to one another. They smiled and were pure and genuine in their words, thanking us with their eyes and outstretched arms.

I humbly stepped off the truck and walked to the side, stepping out of sight. Over come with emotion, I bowed my head and choked back sobs. I was filled with an overwhelming sense of goodness and light.

The rest of that day, I sat and talked with my new friends. I smiled as I watched the children play and laugh amongst nature's devastation. I felt God everywhere. I saw Him in these people.

For that period of time, there were no judgments, no greed and no self-pity.

My journey started with fear and apprehension. Along this path, strangers showed me living examples of Christ. Their actions made me want to be a better person, a better living example of faith.

This experience is forever seared into my memory, into my soul.

Through God's grace I was saved and was changed. Now, I'm ready for His work.

My prayer for you:

❋   ❋   ❋

For it is by grace you have been saved, through faith—and this is not from yourselves, it is the gift of God—not by works, so that no one can boast. For we are God's workmanship, created in Christ Jesus to do good works, which God prepared in advance for us to do.

Dear Jesus, I thank You for Your presence in my life. Without You, I would be filled with fear. You bring ultimate peace and light to my life. Through the examples of others, You show me how You want me to live.

I pray that my eyes will continue to be opened and that my heart will be filled with Your love and Your peace.

This I ask in your name. Amen.

Chapter Three
Strength
❋ ❋ ❋

"I can do everything through Him who gives me strength." Philippians 4:13

I had her life planned out before she was born. I envisioned what she would wear when she was a baby, what she would eat, imagined her personality. I saw her on her first day of school, having a boyfriend, going to college, getting married and having kids of her own some day.

Who doesn't see their little girl this way from the beginning?

But what if this isn't what happens? What if somehow her path takes a different turn? What are you supposed to do then?

Her name is Sarah Grace. She was born on September 22nd weighing in at four pounds exactly. She was 16 inches long and was absolutely beautiful. She had all her fingers and toes and her face reflected features of her brother, sister, mom and dad.

Sarah Grace was born with a genetic disorder that was incompatible with sustained life. In addition, she had a large hole in her heart and underdeveloped lungs.

Despite all this, she proved to have a fighting spirit. She opened her eyes and let out little cries to let her family know she was doing her part to stay with them as long as she could. She wasn't a quitter and neither was her mom.

Having a child who has been diagnosed with any kind of medical condition cements the fact that you are not in control. How do you survive situations like this, when your dreams become derailed?

I've asked this question many times to many different families. The answers, although different in detail, all center on the same main theme: that there is a special plan for their child and they need to rely on their faith to carry them through the difficult times. People generally learn that they need to slow down and take one day at a time in order to be fully *present* in the moment.

The word present is interesting to me. I like it because it actually has three very different meanings, with all of them interconnected with life itself.

The first association I have for the word is its use as a noun, which defines *present* as "a thing presented as a gift." To me, life is a gift. It doesn't matter how short or long that life may last; it is always a gift.

As with any gift, it is *presented* to us by someone who has carefully thought out what we may want, desire or need. This someone is God.

So people ask, "Why would God give us a gift if it will cause us pain?" Who needs a gift like that?

Most people want to feel good and avoid pain and discomfort, physically and emotionally. The reality is that we

Chapter Three: Strength

will have periods of time in our lives where we will suffer from pain and discomfort.

The way to survive these times is to trust that God will be there to meet our needs. Trust isn't always so easy. Sometimes we barter with God, making promises like a child, willing the outcome to be different than what has ultimately been decided.

Megan, Sarah's older sister, told me that her bargain went something like this, "I never took out a book for recreational reading, I paid attention to the teacher in math class, and I worked really hard on all of my push-ups and sit-ups in gym. I told myself that I wouldn't complain about having to practice the piano. I thought that maybe if God saw how hard I was working, then maybe he would let Sarah stay."

Hearing words like this are heartbreaking, as we feel helpless in our ability to change the course of events. It is at these broken moments where we can take time to be present and contemplate the differences between what we want and what we actually need. We may not always get what we want; but we *always* will get what we need.

Sometimes, this means receiving the courage to face death.

Sarah Grace lived for 31 hours. She died surrounded by her family, while being held in her father's arms.

What do you do after a death like this? We do the obvious things like muddle through life like a zombie, cry for hours at a time, look at pictures daily for months on end and then, we become angry.

Angry at the birthday party that is happening in the hospital room next to yours as your baby is dying. Angry at the insensitivity of the doctor who, as she marched out of your room, so bluntly told you that your baby would die. Angry at the "welcome home" message the hospital left you on your answering machine. Angry at the people you thought were your friends, who casually disappeared when you needed them the most.

Anger is a normal reaction and is an emotion that is brought on by intense sorrow.

When this was happening to my friends, they made a choice to continue to trust in God and live by the verse, "I can do everything in Him who gives me strength."

This didn't take away the fact that they had sleepless nights or the fact that they still had two other children who needed their love and attention.

I asked my friend, "Were you ever angry at God for what happened with Sarah?" Her answer was profound.

She said, "I don't remember being angry at God, but I sure questioned, *why?* We wanted this baby. We were good parents and would love this child unconditionally."

She went on to say, "It seemed like there were stories about babies being left in dumpsters or abused every time I watched the news. WHY?"

She prayed to God to give her strength so that she could get through each day. As she did this, she said, "Then, I would remember... God knows what I'm going through... after all, He watched His Son die, too."

My prayer for you:

❋ ❋ ❋

I CAN DO EVERYTHING THROUGH HIM WHO GIVES ME STRENGTH.

THERE ARE TIMES WHEN ALL I HAVE IS YOUR STRENGTH, LORD. LIFE CAN BE REALLY HARD, PAINFUL AND CONFUSING. I NEED YOUR STRENGTH. I NEED HOPE. ACTUALLY, YOU KNOW MY NEEDS AND ALWAYS PROVIDE FOR THEM EXACTLY AT THE RIGHT TIME. THANK YOU FOR UNDERSTANDING MY SORROW AND MY QUESTIONS.

I PRAY THAT YOU WILL CONTINUE TO STRENGTHEN ME SO THAT MY ACTIONS WILL BE AN EXAMPLE TO OTHERS DURING THEIR MOMENTS OF SUFFERING.

IN YOUR NAME I PRAY. AMEN.

Chapter Four
Acceptance
❋ ❋ ❋

"Peace I leave with you; my peace I give you. I do not give to you as the world gives. Do not let your hearts be troubled and do not be afraid." John 14:27

Summer camp is a rite of passage for kids. Some kids look forward to camps that teach new skills like soccer or a musical instrument, while others are mini vacations that allow kids to nurture their carefree sides on water skis, zip lines, and more. And still yet, there is another kind of camp: one that is designed to teach love and self-acceptance to kids who have experienced cancer.

For almost a decade, I was a counselor at one of these camps. I worked specifically with teenagers who were 16 to 19 years old. I worked side-by-side with my trusted friend and co-counselor, training these teenagers to become counselors themselves. She and I made a great team, both having backgrounds in special education. We initially met when she began volunteering at our local children's hospital, and our bond strengthened over humor and sarcasm and the skills each of us brought to the table. For several years, we had worked to create this special program for camp and felt like it was finally becoming solidified.

This year, we would witness a transcendent moment that would shape us all.

Our group consisted of 11 girls and the two of us, our largest group yet. We slept in a one-room cabin, which was filled with six bunk beds, one single bed, one sink, a small shower, one toilet and a furry little mouse.

This little mouse had a huge personality. His favorite game was to come out at night and sit on the small set of shelves, which rested against the wall next to the wooden screened door. This is where we kept our snacks. We knew to keep them in tightly sealed containers, yet somehow, our little friend could find ways to break inside. We would hear him at night, up to his shenanigans, and would shine our flashlights in his direction in hopes of scaring him away. Rather than run off, he would sit up and stare right at our lights with what looked like a grin of mischief in his little beady eyes. It was as if he were saying, "Thanks for the snacks, girls, these are delicious!" He became our cabin "mascot" for the week.

During the unpacking hour that first day, we instituted some of our cabin rules:

>**Rule #1:** Put your suitcases under the bunks to keep the walking space free around the room.

>**Rule #2:** Make sure you zip your suitcases closed, as our friendly mouse liked to hide inside as a surprise. (Yes, this happened to the teenager who slept under my top bunk... that was a loud moment of discovery!)

Chapter Four: Acceptance

Rule #3: To ensure that everyone could enjoy a hot shower, we learned that we had to space them out. Half of the girls showered at night, the other half in the morning.

Rule #4: All perfume, body spray and hair product had to be used on the front porch. (Did someone forget that this was a *camp*? Then again, these are teens we are talking about.)

Rule #5: Have fun!

That summer, the diverse mix of girls, all with their own personalities and insecurities, were strangers to one another.

Upon first glance, our group had a beauty queen, a rebel, a tough tomboy and one who wanted to take her own life. For all of our activities we included the teen boys' cabin, which added another dimension to the group dynamics.

The purpose of our program was to provide a safe and fun atmosphere for learning leadership skills. We held most of our "classes" outside, taking advantage of what nature had to offer.

To set a positive tone and to accomplish our goals for the week, we needed first to build our team. We did this through song, skits, and games.

In the beginning, the kids were tough—tough on each other and even tougher on themselves. They were slow to build friendships, hesitant to let others see behind the protective walls each had built to shield the impact that their cancer had on their life.

They had lost friends because of their long hospital stays and absences from school. They had missed out on participation in sports because their treatments had left their bodies too weak to play. They had missed out on boyfriends, dates, Homecoming and Prom.

They had missed out on life as a regular teen while trying desperately to escape death.

Camp was a place where they could leave all of this behind, a place where they would learn that they weren't alone in their struggles. They were free to be themselves and to relish that reprieve.

The first part of our week, we utilized the ropes courses to teach our group to trust and depend on one another. Starting with the low course, we focused on collaboration. The low ropes elements are close to the ground so the perceived risk is low, but the course is still challenging to complete.

Together, we walked tightropes, negotiated obstacles, climbed walls, and passed teammates through a giant web. To navigate the challenges successfully, each member had to participate. Gradually, through problem solving and the sharing of ideas, each was instinctively able to expand their own comfort zones and recognize the fears that had been blocking their own personal achievements.

At the end of each ropes activity, the group met to discuss the day's successes and their perceptions of the event. After a couple of days, we noticed progress – the campers were becoming aware of inner feelings and what drove them to act and react in certain ways. Self-discovery was beginning to take place.

Chapter Four: Acceptance

Our teens took their newly learned skills and implemented them with younger campers during daily camp activities like swimming, horseback riding, canoeing, archery, art and music. We would regroup in the late afternoons and discuss their experiences that day as junior counselors. We answered questions and provided examples as guidance for their next day's work.

Some of our most important discoveries were revealed during our "forest time." We took our group out into the woods each day to surround them with a "nature-only" scape. We wanted the distractions of camp to fall away for the moment so that they could reflect upon their interactions with one another. We hoped this would enable them to gain personal insight for challenges that may lie ahead.

One day, we had our teens write letters to themselves. We asked them to take their paper and find a spot amongst the trees that spoke to them. We wanted them to include information about their camp experience: why they had made the decision to be at camp that week, how they were feeling about themselves and what they had learned so far. We also wanted them to include a goal they hoped to achieve before heading back home.

These letters were private. We asked the girls to write their home addresses on the provided envelopes so that they could seal them until they were mailed. We let them know that we were going to keep them for a few months and would mail them out when we felt the timing was just right.

During this quiet time, one young lady turned to me and whispered that she didn't know how to address her envelope. She was clearly embarrassed by her disclosure. I asked if she knew what her address was, and she told me yes. I instructed her, "O.K., you just write your address on the front of the envelope so we can mail it to your home."

She looked at me for a minute and continued, "That's the problem. I don't know *where* to write it on the front. I've never been shown how to do this." With confusion, I replied, "What do you mean? No one has ever taught you how to address an envelope? Not even in school? Not even your mom?"

Her answer broke my heart.

She went on to tell me that when she was a little girl, she found out that she had cancer. No one thought she was going to live. She came from a large family and was the youngest of her siblings. After she had her first treatment course, her cancer came back. She had relapsed and from there had to have a bone marrow transplant. Again, they thought she wouldn't survive.

She told me that her parents treated her like she was a fragile doll, and that they wouldn't let her grow up and be a normal teenager. She understood that they were happy she was alive and that was the reason for their caution. She understood that she was different than her brothers and sisters, and that for her, learning came harder than most people her age. She also knew she was capable of many things, yet hadn't been given the chance to try.

Being sheltered and treated like she would break brought to her feelings of insecurity, shame and fear. She had interests and desires like everyone else. She wanted to break free from her restrictions but didn't know how.

Chapter Four: Acceptance

Camp is a place where you learn how to be in control of your experiences. Camp is where you learn to be the person you are meant to become.

So, at that moment I looked her in the eye and said, "Starting today, you are going to learn how to address an envelope, and you'll never have to ask for that to be done for you again." Her smile filled our space for a long while.

That moment was the beginning of a new chapter in her life. For her, camp had just begun!

The next day, we took the group to the stables. We had planned a horseback ride out to an area where we were going to pitch tents and camp outside for the night. This was a special privilege saved for the teen-aged group. As we gathered around the stable area, sizing up the horses, this same young lady approached me.

She told me she was nervous and had never ridden a horse before. She also declared that she wanted to try because she had made a promise to herself that day when we wrote our letters. On that day, she promised to try everything she'd always wanted to do but had never had the chance. She was scared, but she was willing.

As she walked near her horse, the other girls gathered around her. They gave her hugs and told her she was brave. They encouraged her and gave her pointers on how to get up in the saddle, where to hold on and how to hold the reins. They reassured her that the hardest part had happened. Now, it was time to enjoy the ride!

After we all had mounted our horses, we made our way out of the corral and down the path to our campsite. I stayed in the back to make sure everyone arrived safely. I

A Child Shall Lead

watched as our line became orderly and the horse's hooves fell into a rhythm. I zeroed in on the teen that had said she was scared to ride. As if on cue, the horses pace slowed coming to a stop. I watched her body turn slightly in the saddle until she met my gaze. A smile broke free as she exclaimed, "I'm doing it! I'm riding a horse!" I smiled back and said, "Yes, you are!"

"You are amazing! See you at the campsite "

The overnight campout under the stars solidified our group. We worked as a solid team pitching the tents, creating space for the campfires, arranging our supplies and getting ready for our skits. In the evening we had two of our counselor friends join us with guitars and we sang until our voices ached. We shared silly stories while toasting marshmallows in the fire. Under the stars, we learned about each other and ourselves and began forming strong friendships that seemed to help ease the heaviness in our hearts.

In the morning, we broke camp and headed to our high ropes course, which emphasized risk-taking, trust, and coaching. The challenges were higher off the ground and proved to be intimidating for many.

Here, we followed the "Challenge by Choice©" philosophy, where every participant had the choice to experience his or her own success in the context of his or her own comfort level. This philosophy allows for participants to choose not to do something that they feel will endanger them emotionally.

Climbing poles, jumping off of platforms and zipping down the line between trees were thrilling for some, while others enjoyed the entertainment from below. Whether

Chapter Four: Acceptance

they participated in the actual activity or not, all were cheerleaders encouraging their new friends toward success.

I watched throughout the day as my "sheltered" teen made choices to "watch and cheer" time and time again. I wanted desperately for her to take that risk, to allow herself one challenge so that she could see for herself that she could overcome.

My wish came true at the Wall.

The Wall was made of wide wooden planks that were secured together standing about 15 feet high. The front surface was smooth, with neither ropes nor foot pegs to help with climbing. On the backside of the wall, near the top, there was a small platform where 3 people could stand shoulder to shoulder. From there, you had to jump down to the ground approximately 10 feet.

The rules for this activity were simple. The group had to figure out how to get everyone over the Wall safely. From the front side, the group could work in any way they saw fit in order to get their team member up and over the front side of the Wall. Once you were "over" the Wall, you had to stay behind it and not provide any further assistance to the group. This sounded easy, and they were *all* excited to participate.

The caveat was that only one person at a time was allowed to stay on the platform to help lift. Easy, right?

The group began talking through their strategies. Should the boys help all the girls over first? No. Many of the girls said they weren't strong enough to lift the boys up. Should they mix boys and girls up and over to have a variety?

Should they make a pyramid for people to climb up the Wall or should they boost them up with their hands interlocked?

Observing their communication and problem-solving skills, which had blossomed over the week's time, was fascinating. Most everyone was engaged in the discussion, with the exception of my timid teen. She stood, part of the group physically but quickly overlooked, being pushed to the side as she didn't say a word. I could see she was processing everything she saw and heard.

Finally, they had a plan and its execution began. Up and over they went, at first with great ease. For those who had made it over, their confidence grew and their energy flowed—chatter filled the air from behind the Wall.

Soon, there were only three people left that stood in front. Two of them were boys and one was my quiet teen girl. How was this going to work? As far as bodily strength, she was the weakest of the three. The obvious choice was for her and one other boy to hoist the last boy to the top so he could stay at the top and help lift one of them up.

Here is where the problem presented itself:

The choice was for her to be lifted by him and helped over the ledge, which would leave her to pull up the last boy, or for her to be the last one standing and be pulled up and over the top of the Wall. At first, the latter option seemed to make the most sense.

The problem with that choice was the fact that she didn't have the strength or ability in her legs to make the "jump" so that her hands could grab those being outstretched to

Chapter Four: Acceptance

guide her to the top. Her treatment had left her bones and muscles too weak.

The group became quiet. As they all contemplated the options, the acceptance of defeat filled their faces. The teens in the back were not allowed to give advice. Solutions had to come from the last two standing members. They had come so close; almost everyone had made it over the Wall. What were they going to do?

Everyone was quiet. The silence seemed to last forever. Then, in a soft voice she said, "Lift me up first and I'll stand on the platform and pull you up." The facial expressions on the rest of the team showed skepticism, but they didn't say a word. She registered their thoughts and looked the remaining boy in the eye. She said, "I can do it, trust me."

Really, what did they have to lose? They weren't going to succeed if they gave up, so they might as well try. So, he shrugged his shoulders and said, "O.K. Let's go."

The air filled with anticipation. The group from behind the wall stepped out a little toward the sides so they could witness the final play in this game.

We all stood with our eyes glued to that Wall.

With ease, he lifted her body into the hands of the boy on the platform. He gracefully jumped to the ground, leaving her alone, standing at the top. She stood there for a minute as if deep in her thoughts. She straightened her posture and looked directly into her partner's eyes. She smiled and said with confidence, "I can do this. I can lift you up."

He stood for a second and then smiled back and jumped. She reached down and he reached up. Their fingertips grazed and broke apart, causing him to fall back to the ground. All the air escaped our mouths along with groans. He stood back up and said, "Let's try this again." She looked down at him as if seeing no one else and said back, "I've got you this time. I've got you."

In silent anticipation we watched again as he took that leap up. This time, their hands connected and they both hung there clinging to each other. Without warning a slow clapping cadence began with soft chanting from the group. "You can do this, you can do this," they cheered. The chants got louder and the air became filled with positive words of support and encouragement.

As if fueled by their energy, she began to pull. She pulled and he kicked, his tall body writhing and slamming against that Wall. More chants, more claps, more energy. We all stood around them forming a circle beneath their bodies. "Come on, you've got this. You're almost there! Pull! Pull! *Puullll!*"

His body inched its way to the top of that Wall, and as if we were watching in slow motion, we saw him flop to the other side. He stood up next to her and they embraced in a tight hug. Cheers erupted with our thunderous applause. We jumped up and down screaming and laughing, hugging one another in victory.

After a few minutes, our gaze returned to the top of the Wall where these last two teens stood beaming down upon us. The young man turned and said to the once timid girl, "I *knew* you could do this. I knew you would pull me up. You can do anything you set your mind to do!" Having never been encouraged like this before, she turned from him looking out across the trees. She had changed. She emitted a peace from within. This seemingly small exercise was huge in changing her trajectory. Smiling, she said, as if to herself, "I did it! I *really* did it!" As her gaze moved to where we were all standing, she said loudly, with great pride, "This was the most important thing I've ever done in my life! I *did* it!"

There wasn't a dry eye in the woods that day. Tenacity, perseverance and trust prevailed. The fresh air and beauty that surrounded us allowed for a view through a much different lens. None of us would ever forget this extraordinary experience. This was their moment; this was *our* moment, one that would forever be sealed in time.

With the end of camp near, we reflected back upon our week together. We talked openly about the fears the kids had overcome and how their insecurities had dissolved. Confidences that had once slipped away were restored as they learned to laugh, be silly and live with the purity of a child.

Although there were tears in our goodbyes as we watched the bus drive out of camp, they knew they'd hear from us again. When we mailed the letters that had been written to themselves that first couple days of camp, we included one of our own. We wrote about how we watched them all week. How we saw their struggles to trust one another and themselves. We watched them battle old wounds and slowly mend them so that they could move forward in the healing process.

We described to each one the gifts they possessed and how we witnessed them while they helped out their new friends. Transformation had occurred. Scared, tired, confused little beings blossomed into courageous, joyful souls who gained new hope that there would be a future for each to enjoy and live.

> ## My prayer for you:
> ❈   ❈   ❈
>
> PEACE I LEAVE WITH YOU; MY PEACE I GIVE YOU. I DO NOT GIVE TO YOU AS THE WORLD GIVES. DO NOT LET YOUR HEARTS BE TROUBLED AND DO NOT BE AFRAID.
>
> CIRCUMSTANCES SHAPE WHO WE ARE AND WHO WE BECOME. MANY TIMES, WE ARE NOT IN CONTROL OF WHAT CIRCUMSTANCES WE WILL FACE. THAT CAN BE SCARY AND DISHEARTENING. HOWEVER, WE KNOW THAT WE ALWAYS HAVE A CHOICE IN HOW WE HANDLE THESE CIRCUMSTANCES.
>
> LORD, I ASK THAT YOU GUIDE US TOWARD PEOPLE AND PLACES THAT WILL LEAD TO OUR EMPOWERMENT. HELP US TO TAKE SAFE RISKS SO THAT WE CAN LIVE OUT THE LIFE YOU HAVE INTENDED FOR US.
>
> THESE THINGS I LIFT UP TO YOU IN PRAYER. AMEN.

Chapter Five
Bullies

❋ ❋ ❋

"Don't let anyone look down on you because you are young, but set an example for the believers in speech, in life, in love, in faith and in purity." 1 Timothy 4:12

Hiding deep down inside his sweatshirt, a hood pulled over his head, he is ashamed about something that he had no choice in. He was born with an illness. And, although that clearly wasn't his fault, adults, kids and his school treat him as though it were. He tells me: "I am afraid to tell you what happens to me at school."

"...I don't want them to know I said anything."

"...It's not really that bad, I've learned how to deal with it."

"...I just ignore them and walk away."

"...I am always alone, and that is just the way it is."

As he talks, his voice is small and weak. I have to lean in to hear him speak. He doesn't want to look at me when he says these things. His body shows defeat, his words show fear, and when he does look at me for that rare moment, his eyes show sorrow.

"How can I help you?" I say with empathy in my voice. "What is it that you want them to understand?"

Through a whisper I hear, "Explain to my class, my teacher and my school what I have and why I have to do what I do; *please*."

I am determined to do just that. I ask if he wants to be a part of this awareness training, the education to help everyone understand a day in his life? Surprisingly, without hesitation, he answers, "Yes." For the rest of his visit, we discuss his goal and the outcome he hopes we could achieve.

Step one: Create a slide show of pictures that discuss his illness, how it impacts his body and the treatments he needs each day... in order to survive. A slide at the end will show his personal interests, in hopes that his classmates will find that they weren't that different after all.

Step two: Arrange a time and date with the classroom teacher so that we can present this slide show to his peers.

Step three: Execute the plan.

One month later...

When I arrived at the school, I saw his dad waiting for me in the office. I signed in and asked how things were going since we last spoke. He answered with a shrug and said, "Things are O.K., but I'm really glad you are here to do this today."

We walked to the classroom where the students were cleaning up, quickly getting ready for our presentation. I stopped at the desk of my student and whispered, "Do you still want to stand up in front of the class with me and help me present, or would you rather sit and listen with your class?"

"I'm with you," he said, and we walked together to the front of the room.

As the introduction began, I noticed a nervous pacing from my friend. I looked around the room and it didn't take me long to figure out which kids were the ones who said the cruel words and taunted him on the playground. The smug attitudes and body posture gave them away.

As each slide clicked, his nerves melted away and the true personality of my student emerged. His peers started to listen and it wasn't long before we had captured their full attention. Even the bullies had settled down and were leaning in to hear more.

We talked about his illness and the genetics behind it. It's amazing how a little science and some props can captivate an audience. We showed equipment and demonstrations of his treatments. Pictures of the hospital guided them through a tour. Surprise registered when we told them that even kids who are in the hospital have to go to school and do their homework! Questions were asked enthusiastically and my friend was flawless in his answers.

I saw transformation beginning to take place.

The final slide, the one noting his hobbies and interests, was a hit. We found out that the majority of the class had the same favorite sport, subject and foods. Laughter ensued as he shared his favorite song. Despite his best imitation, it was only the three adults in the room who rocked out in unison with him.

There were two items on the slide that intrigued the crowd. One, his playing the guitar and two, his interest and skill in origami.

We left time for questions, and by the end of our presentation, we felt some attitudes had changed. We wouldn't know how much until later.

Three months later...

It was time for his check-up in the clinic. As I entered the room I noticed something different in the air. Dad was beaming from ear to ear. I looked at my young friend and he was sitting tall and proud, without a hooded sweatshirt in sight.

I asked how things had been since our presentation to his class. His smiles told me the answer. In excitement, his Dad blurted out, "He has friends! He really has friends!"

"Tell me about that," I said as I looked to my friend. He asked me if I remembered the last slide in our presentation. "Of course," I said.

"Remember when people were asking me about my origami?"

"Yes."

"Well, they wanted to know how I knew how to do it, so I told them that I read about it in a book that I had checked out from the library." His dad started laughing and added, "So the next day, those kids went to the library and checked out every single book they had on origami."

"Wow, that is amazing! Then what?" I asked.

"We needed to find paper. We had used all the scrap paper from our classroom and we were running out of supply."

Dad chimed in again and went on to tell me that one of the teachers in the school asked if his son would start an Origami Club so that all the students who were interested could learn.

Chapter Five: Bullies

This club changed this boy's life. All kinds of kids joined his new Origami Club. The school even found funds to buy the special origami paper.

But here is the best part: With a seriousness and responsibility inflected in his tone, I heard my young friend say, "The best part of this is that there are kids who come to our club who have special needs. They are smart and all but have physical needs that make it hard for them to write and play a lot. They come to my club and *I* get to help them learn. Guess what else?" he said with a note of pride.

"What?" I whispered while choking back a tear.

"They are really, really good at it. Origami is helping them with all of the things they couldn't do before. Their teacher even said she never would have thought of this, and asked if I would keep this club going all year!"

Four months earlier, this young boy had walked into our clinic ashamed and afraid. Today, he walked out a teacher and leader.

My prayer for you:

❊ ❊ ❊

DON'T LET ANYONE LOOK DOWN ON YOU BECAUSE YOU ARE YOUNG, BUT SET AN EXAMPLE FOR THE BELIEVERS IN SPEECH, IN LIFE, IN LOVE, IN FAITH AND IN PURITY.

SO OFTEN WE UNDERESTIMATE THE TRUE ABILITIES OF INDIVIDUALS AROUND US SIMPLY BASED ON OUR IGNORANCE AND NAIVETÉ. THIS CREATES LIMITS INSTEAD OF GROWTH.

GOD, I PRAY THAT YOU ALLOW US TO VALUE EVERYONE THAT WE INTERACT WITH, SO THAT THE GIFTS THAT YOU HAVE EMBEDDED WITHIN THEM CAN BE BROUGHT FORTH TO HELP ALL OF US BECOME IMPROVED PEOPLE.

I PRAY THIS IN YOUR NAME. AMEN.

CHAPTER SIX
Joy
❋ ❋ ❋

*"Therefore my heart is glad and my tongue
rejoices; my body also will rest secure."*
Psalm 16:9

I leave my office heading to the elevator. The halls are empty, a rare sight. Out of nowhere I hear, "Hello!" squeaking out of the mouth of a little 4-year-old girl. This girl is a patient of ours; I can tell by her hospital gown and her plastic medical identification band that wraps around her tiny wrist.

I look around and wonder, *Is she talking to me?*

"Hello!" she squeaks again as I see her brown, bobbed hair bounce directly toward me with unbridled enthusiasm.

"Well, hello to you, young lady!" I say. Her smile is infectious and brightens up the hallway where we are both standing. She stops in front of me, looks into my eyes and asks, "Are you a nurse?"

"No," I say, "I am a teacher."

A gasp escapes her mouth and her smile broadens even farther. "A teacher! Oh, goodie! Come with me!" she exclaims as she grabs my hand and starts walking me down the hall.

I can't help but follow. Holding her hand was like wonder in my heart. Curious, I ask, "Where are we going?"

"Oh, we are just going on a walk," she says.

We take off down the hall, as if we are going to leave the Pediatrics floor, when we suddenly turn to the left and continue walking down another hall that parallels the one where we started. We were walking as if we had a mission.

We continue this pattern over and over down each connecting hall. All the while, our arms are swinging in cadence and we are cheerfully greeting everyone we see along the way.

I really am taken aback, as I don't even know who this little girl is, but I want to be around her. She makes people feel special.

I took a moment and looked down at this happy, smiling, precious little bundle of joy, and I said to her, "You are so darn *cute*!" She looked up at me without missing a beat, smiled and said, "And you you are *so* beautiful!"

This took me by surprise. It stopped me in my tracks. What did she just say? It wasn't so much the words she used, rather the way she articulated them.

It was as if time stood still for just a moment. I gazed into her eyes and for a second, the world all made sense. It was as if she knew something really important. Wisdom stared back at me through her bright brown eyes. *Who was she?* I wondered.

Where was her mother? Her father? Why was she walking these halls alone, yet not a bit afraid? She was full of

Chapter Six: Joy

life, transcending goodness and peace. She stared back as if we were sharing a secret. She made me want to know what that secret was and how she understood the power of this secret at such a young age.

Her eyes sparkled with delight and our hands slowly began to release. She told me she had to go back to her room so her mom wouldn't get worried. I felt a small pang of sadness as she turned and walked away. I didn't want her to leave. Her presence calmed me.

I stood for another second just savoring the experience, watching her. I turned and went on my way knowing I had been changed for the better by a brief interaction with a joyful 4-year-old girl.

I never found out her name, but that doesn't matter. She made a mark on my heart that can never be erased. Thank you, my little "Happy Heart." Your actions, your spirit and your kindness to a stranger showed me how I want to be.

Joy:

We all have people in our lives that we want to be around. Think about the reason for that. Do you want to be around them because they make you feel special? Are they gentle in nature or kind to others? Do they have a great sense of humor and make you laugh out loud?

Regardless of the reason, the quality lies within their attitude. People like to be around positive, joyful people.

Joy is often used synonymously with happiness. In actuality, joy goes deeper than happiness. Happiness is based on external circumstances; therefore, it is temporary.

Joy is an inward attitude. True joy is at the soul level. It is lasting because it is based on God's presence *within* us. As we understand that God's presence is with us on a daily basis wherever we go and wherever we are, we will find contentment.

God has promised to be active in our lives at all times. He is all-loving. As we start to believe this and understand the future *He* has for us, we will experience joy.

I saw this joy in a 4-year old girl who walked the halls of our hospital. She made me want to walk with a positive attitude in my heart, filled with the acceptance of God. She made me want to show others my secret.

If someone saw you walking the halls, how would they characterize you?

Would they see mere happiness, or would they see *joy*?

My prayer for you:

❋ ❋ ❋

THEREFORE MY HEART IS GLAD AND MY TONGUE REJOICES; MY BODY ALSO WILL REST SECURE.

IN TODAY'S EVER CHANGING, FAST-PACED WORLD, WE GRAVITATE TOWARD INSTANT HAPPINESS. WHAT WILL MAKE US HAPPY THE FASTEST? HAPPINESS IS BASED ON THESE EXTERNAL CIRCUMSTANCES, BUT IT'S JOY THAT WE ACTUALLY SEEK. WE CAN'T TRULY BE HAPPY UNLESS WE ARE JOYFUL.

Chapter Six: Joy

GOD, I PRAY TODAY THAT YOU WILL GIVE US THE POWER OF DISCERNMENT SO THAT WE CAN EASILY IDENTIFY BETWEEN HAPPINESS AND JOY. HELP GUIDE OUR ACTIONS AND BEHAVIORS SO THAT WE CAN LEAVE A LASTING, POSITIVE IMPRESSION ON THOSE WHO CROSS OUR PATH. WE WANT OUR EYES TO EMIT THAT JOY SO THAT OTHERS WILL WANT TO KNOW YOU.

I PRAY THIS IN YOUR NAME. AMEN.

Chapter Seven
Hope

❋   ❋   ❋

"Then the eyes of the blind be opened and the ears of the deaf unstopped. Then will the lame leap like a deer, and the mute tongue shout for joy." Isaiah 35:5-6

When you work with people, especially children, there is a question that passes through your mind, occasionally taunting it, asking, "Are you really doing anything that will matter to this child or that will have a lasting impact on their life?"

Many years ago, I got a surprising answer to this question. Eleven-year-old Leslie was a student of mine with cystic fibrosis. Leslie was full of life, emitting an energy that was contagious. She could bring a smile to your face even on your worst day. Her eyes held a sparkle that let you know that she had a purpose in everything she did. She was courageous and witty and wanted to try all that life had to offer.

August

We called ourselves "soul sisters," and I truly believed we were. It started with our discovery that our birthdays were only days apart. We both loved the ocean, the grace of the dolphins and the color purple.

We also both had the personality trait of being entertainers. Many days found us singing country music and dancing together around her hospital room. I would bring in the CD player and plug it in with her favorite country songs ready to play. We would decide the song order and pick which parts we'd sing. I'd scan the room to see what we could use as our props. Sometimes, a hairbrush or even a pen could be transformed into a microphone. IV poles turned into guitars and beds became our stage.

For the duration of those songs, life in the hospital went away. Leslie was able to be a young girl who could be silly, dance and find freedom from her illness.

The days I knew that Leslie was in the hospital were my favorite days to go to work. I would get up in the morning and on my drive in, I would plan what we would do that day.

Our classroom was a little different than one you might see in a typical school. Space is always a commodity in a hospital, and our classroom had a unique wavy shape to it, as it at one time had been a linen closet. There was only one flush wall where our computers rested. The largest wall was curved and held two beautifully oval-shaped windows that gave us a view of the mountains and the city.

In the center of the room near the two windows, we had a table and several chairs. Everyone had to share that space to work. That was difficult at times, especially when we were fitting wheelchairs, oxygen tanks and suction machines underneath or near the table.

Chapter Seven: Hope

On the wall closest to the table, we had panels that let me plug in oxygen hoses for those students who needed it. That saved the oxygen in their tanks so that they could roam outside their room a little longer. Depending on how much oxygen was needed, one tank could usually last for up to two hours.

Our last wall space was a shelving unit that had doors attached. The shelves held all of our materials, and the doors, when closed, acted as our display board, white board and sign holder. The door to our classroom had a window, which was great for the nurses, doctors and families, as they could watch what we were doing in school without interrupting our discussions.

Leslie loved to write, and she loved to do science experiments. More than that, she loved to socialize with the other kids in the classroom. "What are you here for?" she would ask. "Who is your favorite nurse? Isn't the food here totally gross?"

I would say to her, "Leslie, you need to focus on your work so everyone else can focus on theirs." She would look up at me with her award-winning smile and say, "I know, I know," and then she would obediently get back to her work.

March

Leslie and I also shared a love for Dr. Seuss. One year, she happened to be in the hospital when we were celebrating Dr. Seuss's birthday. One of our activities involved kids singing a newly-made school song to the staff at the hospital.

As I was setting up for our event, Leslie, with her oxygen tank tagging along behind her, asked me, "Miss Carla, I have always wanted to be a cheerleader and because of my stupid illness and me being in and out of the hospital all of the time, I will never get the chance to be one. Do you think that I could be a cheerleader today for our celebration, just for a little bit, for our school song?"

I didn't miss a beat, responding with an excited, "Of course! Let me go find you your pompoms." I raced away, praying that I would have something in my closet that would resemble a pompom. My prayers were answered. I reached inside my closet and brought out two obnoxious orange pompoms. They were a little on the thin side, small wooden sticks with just a few plastic orange shreds that could pass as streamers glued to the top, but they were perfect!

As I walked back to the hallway where I had put up the words to our song, I saw Leslie there reading the words to herself, practicing her cheer movements that she had created just for this moment.

I stopped for a moment to watch and absorb this moment in its entirety. I smiled as I walked toward her and when I handed her the bright orange, silly looking, thin pompoms, she let out a squeal of joy, jumped up and down and started shaking away.

Suddenly she stopped, looked up at me and said in her most matter-of-fact voice that for the "real" performance she was not going to be wearing her oxygen and that was that. "I see," I stated. In my mind I told myself that it would only be for 5 minutes, and I'd just keep that little tidbit of information between her and me. Neither the respiratory therapists nor the doctors needed to know. She wanted to be just like a "real" cheerleader, even if it was just for that one moment in time.

I ran to get my camera so that I could document her performance. The pictures are rarely for me; rather, they are for the parents, to be given as a keepsake. Some have asked, "Why take pictures of a child in the hospital? Isn't that morbid?" I would answer by asking, "Is it morbid to chronicle your child's life events? To capture their story, whatever that might be? Wherever that might take place?"

I take pictures for parents who can't be present to witness the happy times that are often intermixed with the tragic ones. For this moment in time, with Leslie being our school's cheerleader and the rest of the kids singing our song to the staff, it felt like the walls that surrounded us were those of a "regular" school building, rather than walls that surrounded a hospital for kids.

September

During another hospital admission during the school year, Leslie had a science project due for her school's science fair. "How unfair!" she screamed. "I always have to miss out on everything because of my stupid disease!" She was angry, and rightly so.

Tears streamed down her emotion-reddened face. I looked her in the eye and stated in a determined tone, "You don't have to miss out on anything, Leslie. We'll do your experiment here." That stopped her tears and she stared at me quizzically.

At first she was skeptical, wondering both how we'd get the materials (her experiment was baking four batches of chocolate chip cookies, leaving out a different ingredient for each batch) and how we'd fit in the time to bake between her medical treatments. I am sure she also questioned where we might actually bake cookies in a children's hospital. "Leave the details to me," I urged. "I just need you to trust that we can get this done and I need you to commit to your part 100 percent. Can you do that?" I asked. She held her head high and answered with a resounding, "Of course!"

After several days of making calls to hospital department heads, gathering bowls, spoons and cookie sheets, and shopping for all of our needed ingredients, we were ready to start.

I had reserved the adult therapy kitchen in the building next door to our hospital, gained doctors' permission to leave the floor for a couple of hours, and rearranged all of her therapy and medicines with her nursing and respiratory staff. This was no small feat!

We had exactly three hours of time to get there, bake and get back. The nurses laughed at us as they saw me pushing Leslie in a wheelchair, oxygen tank strapped on the back, IV pole hooked up to one arm, and a wagon filled with bowls, spoons, pans and ingredients trailing behind us.

Exactly three hours later, after baking four batches of cookies and taking a camera full of silly pictures, we were done with *Step 1* of her experiment. Next, was *Step 2*, the "taste test" conducted by the doctors and staff. This went well. Leslie had each of the four batches of cookies

Chapter Seven: Hope

on plates. She made signs that read, "Batch 1," "Batch 2," "Batch 3," and "Batch 4." She created a scoring card with questions and a rating scale so that participating staff could rank their favorites and why.

After the taste test was completed, Leslie was ready for *Step 3* of her experiment, which was tallying and writing up the results. Unfortunately, before she could do so, Leslie's illness worsened and she was no longer able to leave her bed. Her goal was to finish this science project by the school's deadline.

I came to her room daily, wheeling a computer bedside so that I could type up her results as she dictated to me while lying in her bed on her back, unable to even sit. I would send the typed drafts to my office printer, retrieve them and then lay them out on a board for her to review.

I remember having to stand on the end of her bed holding the science board up at an angle so that she could critique the details of her papers, while she remained on her back with tubes hanging out of her chest.

Talk about perseverance. It was humbling to be in her presence. Once Leslie felt like her science project was suitable for submission, I drove it down to her school.

Obviously, she wasn't able to be at her school in person to discuss her project, so she planned ahead, answering questions she thought might be asked and including those questions and answers in her display.

Her classroom teacher called me and asked me how Leslie had managed to get this project done. I explained our conversations, Leslie's desire to be a part of this project and her persistence and dedication to her goals.

Leslie's hard work paid off! She received a blue ribbon at her school's science fair. Her teacher allowed me to come to the school and collect her board with the award-winning ribbon so that I could display it in Leslie's room at the hospital.

When I walked through her door, Leslie propped herself up onto her elbow. It was if the sun had broken through a tunnel sealed from light. Her eyes danced as she saw the large blue ribbon hanging from the corner of her board. She giggled and her smile stretched across the width of her face.

"We did it!" she whispered, her lungs not allowing for a full breath of air. "No," I said softly. "*You* did this. You set a goal, committed to it 100 percent and, despite all of your obstacles, you got this done. *You* did this and I am so very proud of you! Thank you for allowing me to be standing here with you sharing in your success."

I held back my tears as I set her board up near her window. I wanted everyone that walked into her room to see what she had been able to accomplish and to have the opportunity to talk about it with her.

January

One month turned into the next, and I began to get the dreadful feeling that Leslie wasn't going to ever leave the hospital. Her health was declining at a rapid rate.

Discussions started taking place within the cystic fibrosis team about the potential of a lung transplant. This transplant would be Leslie's only chance for longer-term survival. Maybe she could survive another five years?

Chapter Seven: Hope

Because of my special bond with Leslie, her parents had asked that I sit in with them on all of the meetings surrounding a lung transplant and any other medical issues that pertained to her. This was an honor and a privilege, one I didn't take lightly.

As days passed, I knew there would be a time when Leslie would have to spend what little energy she had on breathing and not take this energy to talk, so I started teaching her sign language. I told her this was a way we could still communicate. I spent time each day sitting by her side, teaching her the alphabet and various simple signs. Leslie enjoyed these lessons. She always wanted to learn new things. But despite this drive, her body was beginning to give up. Leslie was becoming tired.

April

One day, as I was spending time in Leslie's room, she said to me, using great effort, "Miss Carla, my mom and I have the best present for you, but I can't tell you what it is." I said, "Leslie, you don't need to give me a present." She responded, "No, this is better than a present, but I can't tell you what it is yet."

Didn't she know that *she* was the best present I could ever have and that her mother gave me that gift by allowing me to become part of their lives? As I left her room, her comment left the forefront of my mind. I was too consumed with figuring out how to make her time in the hospital productive and positive.

The cryptic message she was trying to convey had found a place in a drawer tucked deeply in the back of my mind.

A Child Shall Lead

It was only a few days later, a Friday, when I was sitting on Leslie's bed face to face with her. I told her that I was going to be coming to the hospital on Saturday (which was not normally a day I worked) to help with a hospital tour. I said that I was excited because that meant that I got to see her one extra day that week. We did a few signs, and then we sat in silence for what seemed like a very long time.

I felt as though she was contemplating something quite serious. I felt like she wanted me to know her thoughts as she tried to figure out the exact words to say. I wanted to ask what it was that she was thinking, but I couldn't bring myself to speak those words, even though I knew in my gut what was to be the truth.

I thought that if I didn't say the words out loud then they wouldn't be true. "One more day," I prayed silently. "Please, just one more day." She put her arm around me and let out a sigh as I bent down to kiss her cheek goodbye. I told her that I would come see her in the morning as I forced a smile, winked and walked out the door, closing it behind me.

That day was the last time I saw Leslie awake. The next morning as I arrived to work, I was told that Leslie was in our Intensive Care Unit and that she didn't have much time. I waited with her family, friends and staff as she struggled to fight the illness that was taking her life.

I walked into the ICU staring at our doctors who were hunched over charts, desperately trying to find something that they could do to stop her dying process.

My insides were shaking as I approached her room. I saw her parents, sister and other family members standing around awkwardly, cramming themselves into the corners

Chapter Seven: Hope

of a much-too-small room trying not to intrude on the one whose turn it was to sit on her bed.

They tried not to look at the monitors, the machines and the faces of the others, but they couldn't ignore the beeps, the weeping and the tears. Then it was my turn.

I was given the privilege of spending some time with her, next to her on her bed, as she lay in her deep sleep. As I approached her, the room fell silent. It was like everyone was holding their breath. I noticed the staff in the hall had stopped what they were doing and looked up at me, too, holding my gaze as I inched closer to Leslie.

I could feel their stares on my back as I sat down. It took every ounce of strength I had not to break down and wail. I took a deep breath and exhaled it, and then I leaned over so that my mouth was next to Leslie's ear.

I whispered to her gently, letting her know how much she was loved by me and by all those around her. I held her hand and stroked her hair as tears streamed down my face. I sat there not wanting to get up, not wanting to let go, not wanting to turn around and look into her parents' eyes.

After a few more minutes and another deep breath, I slowly stood and turned around, shaking from my very core.

Her mom came to my side and embraced me, telling me that while I whispered in Leslie's ear, her heart rate increased as if she understood what I was telling her. "Talk to her again, maybe she'll come back to us," she pleaded.

I knew this wasn't true, but how do you tell this to a grieving parent? I encouraged everyone in the room to take their turn telling Leslie stories, talking to her and letting her know how much she was loved.

A Child Shall Lead

I took another turn, and it was then that I witnessed the moment her last breath left her body. It seemed surreal. Her fight was over. She could now run, cheer, jump and do all of the things she always wanted to do but never could. How lucky the heavenly angels were to get her.

Despair filled the hearts of the family who were left behind and there to witness the end. Some left the room, as it was too hard to watch.

Leslie's mom, dad and sister were standing with me as the doctors and nurses turned the machines down, then off and quietly unhooked them from Leslie's body. "What do we do next?" they asked me. I let them know the process of what happens in the hospital after a death. They would have as much time as they needed with Leslie's body to say goodbye. Someone would need to call the funeral home and make arrangements. Handprints could be made if they wanted that memory of her. The nurses would arrange the bed, putting a soft blanket around her to make her look like she was sleeping peacefully. I would stay there so they wouldn't have to do this alone.

Once the funeral home had been called and a time arranged for them to come get Leslie's body, her mom turned to me and said, "I can't be here any longer. This is too hard. I need to go." I nodded, not having any words to say. "I don't want her to be alone. I can't bear that thought," she said with a broken voice. "Please," she begged. "Please stay with her until they take her away."

"Of course," I managed to squeak out, thinking there would be other staff there, too, as I'd never been with a

Chapter Seven: Hope

child after she had died. Mom left and there I stood, alone in a quiet room with Leslie.

She looked so peaceful and beautiful. The sun came through the window and made the room feel warm. No one entered the room.

I continued to stand right where I was, just watching. I think I was hoping to see a miracle, that somehow the doctors were wrong, that the machines were somehow broken and that, suddenly, Leslie would start breathing again, open her eyes, smile and say, "Why are you looking at me that way?"

Of course, that's not what happened.

Instead, I waited until I saw the coroner from the funeral home. He came into the room with a stretcher on wheels and had a large black bag with him. It hadn't occurred to me what that might be for.

He greeted me with a shy hello and seemed to be timid in what he needed to do. I told him my name and Leslie's name as well. I explained that her parents had left the hospital but had asked me to wait with her until he arrived.

As he was preparing to lift Leslie out of the hospital bed onto the stretcher, he started asking me questions about her life. He wanted to know a little bit about her. He wanted to humanize her, and for that, I was grateful.

He was kind and he told me the reason he seemed timid when he first walked into the room was that Leslie was a child. "It's never easy when it's a child," he offered.

That was when I saw it. The large black bag. I suddenly understood its purpose.

My eyes grew wide and immediately filled with tears as I looked from the stretcher to this man, pleading "No!" without saying a word.

His face softened even more and he asked me if I wanted to say goodbye one last time. I choked back a sob, leaned down to cradle Leslie's face, and I gently kissed her head as this stranger and I both zipped the bag closed.

Leslie's funeral took place in the cafeteria of her community school. It was beautifully decorated, with pictures of her from birth to just before her death.

There were posters that her friends had made, telling us what they remembered and liked most about Leslie. Her science fair poster and blue ribbon were displayed, representing the determination and dedication to her goals.

Songs were sung and words spoken letting the world know how powerfully impacted they had been and how lessons were gained by just being in the presence of this young girl.

She was buried beneath a statue of an angel holding a child in her arms. I like to think that this is how Leslie was received into Heaven—within the arms of an angel.

July

A few months after Leslie's death, I received a letter in the mail stating that I had been nominated for a very prestigious teaching award. A student had nominated me for this. The student was Leslie.

The nomination was her "surprise." The one she couldn't tell me about that day in her hospital room. That cryptic

Chapter Seven: Hope

message I had stored away was now presenting itself before my eyes and the puzzle was being solved.

What a bittersweet gift to receive. I cried tears of joy, for I had been blessed with knowing her. I cried tears of sorrow, as I couldn't thank her for my gift. I cried tears of anger that such a dear young life had been taken away so soon. I laughed through my tears, as I finally understood what she was trying to tell me on that day.

I became one of the finalists in the awards and I had the privilege to travel to Los Angeles for the celebration.

While entering my hotel, I heard a song playing overheard. It was Leslie's and my favorite song. The one we sang endlessly in her hospital room while we danced around with hairbrush microphones.

I stopped for a minute, closed my eyes smiling, listening until the song ended. I like to think that was Leslie's way of saying hello. I like to think it was my chance to say, "Thank you."

The gift she had given me goes beyond her "surprise." That was just the beginning. The true gift is the realization that I had not been the teacher all of those years, rather, the one who had been taught. Thank you, Leslie. I will treasure this gift forever and pass it along to others so that they, too, can receive.

Hope:
The story doesn't end here.

When I became a finalist for this award, Disney sent a camera crew and staff to the hospital where I worked to film a "day in the life" of a hospital teacher.

After over 10 hours of filming, each finalist was given a 2-3 minute clip of their teaching, their students and parent interviews, to be shown the night of the award ceremony.

I asked Leslie's mom if she would be comfortable and willing to share her insights about Leslie while she was part of our school program. She graciously agreed. Despite being nervous to be on camera and not comfortable with the attention she was getting, she gave a strong and uplifting testimony.

There was one statement she made that was so powerful, I have never forgotten the words. She looked directly at the camera and said, "...for Leslie to be part of this school program while she was in the hospital, it was like the hope for tomorrow was never gone...."

Being a part of something normal, like school, gave Leslie hope and gave her mom hope, too. It made all the uncomfortable, scary and sad parts of their day disappear, even if just for a few hours at a time.

Hope is strong. It carries people through experiences like nothing else is able to do. Hope also graces us with time. Time to accept, time to reflect and time to make choices.

As if God wasn't present before, He made Himself *known* within the year of Leslie's death. It was months later when Leslie's mom called me and told me she started going to church.

At first, this took me by surprise, as I hadn't known her to be much of a "church" person. I was curious to know what prompted the change, so I asked. She told me that she had seen how many people Leslie had touched during her short life and knew that God clearly had His hand in that.

Chapter Seven: Hope

She told me about the generous support that the people in her local community had offered to her and how many of these people attended the church nearby. She said she often wanted to go to the church but felt like she would be judged or wouldn't fit in somehow.

After meeting some of these people, along with the pastor, she changed her mind and decided to try one service. She said that she walked in and sat in the very front row! How's that for embracing the love?

I congratulated her on her courage, because it is scary and can be uncomfortable to go to a place where you might think people won't accept who you are or understand where you've been. I told her how happy I was for her.

The next words out of her mouth brought tears to my eyes. She said, "I have decided that I am going to be baptized, and I want you to be there as a witness."

Chills ran over my body, forming goosebumps on my arms. I blurted out, "Of course!" while feeling humbled and honored by her request. The day of her baptism, she welcomed me to sit with her family, in that front row!

She had requested several pieces of music to be played and sung, some of which were Leslie's favorites and some of which were hers. It was a joyous, uplifting celebration!

After the baptism, I checked in periodically with Leslie's mom, but our daily conversations started turning weekly, and then monthly. I knew she still grieved for her daughter and that she also hid her pain well. I thought of her and her husband often, but time, as it does, continued to move along.

Several months had passed and I was traveling out of state for a work-related conference. I boarded the plane and took my seat next to the window. I like window seats because they allow me to look out and see the sky, the weather and the clouds. For some reason, this brings me peace and helps pass the time between destinations.

This particular trip, I was emotionally tired from all that had happened with work and my students. I rested my head on my seat back and closed my eyes. Within minutes, I felt as though I was being yanked out of my seat and right out of my body.

I had read about things like this, these "out of body" experiences, yet had never had one myself before now.

I found myself standing in front of this large, black space. I was alone and watching very bright, neon-colored lights dance before me in shapes similar to numbers and letters. There was no semblance to them and what I seemed to notice most were their vibrant colors.

From somewhere behind this black curtain of space, I heard Leslie's voice. I knew without a doubt who it was. She was telling me to come closer and I could hear her plain as day.

I reached a point where I couldn't walk any farther toward her. The space became a barrier that I could not forge. I bent down trying to see her underneath. I tried to peer at her around a side, as if this space were a curtain that I could manipulate. It was not. It was solid, yet undefined.

Leslie told me that I would not be able to see her, so I should stop trying to find a way around. However, I'd be able to hear her.

Chapter Seven: Hope

I stood back up and kept talking to her. I asked her several rapid-fire questions: "Where are you? Why can't I see you? How are you? Are you happy?"

I told her that there were so many people that loved her and missed her. I told her I wanted to give her a hug!

She giggled and I could sense her smiling through her words. She told me that she was happy and in a wonderful place. She told me she knew people loved her and that she didn't want them to be sad for her. She told me she knew her mom cried a lot for her and she wanted me to give her a message.

I said, "Sure, I'll tell your mom anything you want me to. What is it?" She said she wanted me to be her messenger. She wanted me to tell her mom that she was happy and in a good place. She wanted her mom to know this without a doubt. She also told me to tell her mom to stop crying for her, her crying was tearing her up, and she wanted her mom to know that she was O.K.! She wanted me to tell her mom that she loved her, too.

I said, "O.K., I will tell her that for sure!" Leslie said, "You promise to tell her?" I said, "Of course."

Without warning, as if on cue, I was being sucked back out of this space. I had a sense of falling, yet I wasn't afraid. *Slam!* I was thrown back into my body and back into my seat on the plane.

I jerked open my eyes and had my hand pressed to the seat in front of me. I looked around, just knowing someone next to me had seen my body flying around and getting yanked in and out of the seat.

To my surprise, no one was looking at me. In fact, it was like they didn't notice anything at all. My heart was racing. I looked around the plane, straightened my seatbelt and looked out the window feeling perplexed.

What had just happened to me? Had I really just talked to Leslie? I continued to stare out the airplane window trying to absorb what I had just been a part of, trying to explain it to myself and wondering what I was supposed to do with that experience. Would I actually tell Leslie's mom of my experience?

I have to admit that it took me about a month to call her. I kept wondering if she was going to think I was "crazy" or something. Seriously, how do you call someone up and say, "Oh, by the way, a funny thing happened to me while I was on an airplane last month. I had a really nice conversation with your dead daughter."

I found myself picking up my phone, starting to dial and then hanging up before it could ring. I questioned myself daily. I wasn't questioning whether I truly had spoken with Leslie, because I knew this to be true. I questioned if whether or not my message to Leslie's mom would hurt her further or help ease her pain.

I was scared that she might be angry with me for telling her that I talked to Leslie and thought she might resent the fact that she didn't. This went on for weeks.

Finally, I summoned the courage to make the call. After all, I had made a promise.

I picked up my phone and dialed Leslie's mom's number. While it was ringing, I stood in my kitchen praying to God that He give me the right words to say to her, so as to

Chapter Seven: Hope

comfort her and not hurt her. Then, I heard her voice say, "Hello?"

With my heart racing and my palms sweating, I swallowed and said, "Hi! This is Carla." She sounded relieved and happy.

"Well, it's about time!" she proclaimed loudly. "You have a message for me from Leslie, don't you?"

I practically screamed into the phone, "How did you know that?" I started jumping up and down in my kitchen and talking a mile a minute. We both were sobbing and laughing and trying to not talk over each other.

After a deep breath I asked again, "How did you know?" and she told me that she also had talked to Leslie and she had told her that I would be calling her with a message for her.

I apologized for taking so long to call. I explained my hesitations and wondered how she'd react. She told me that she knew of all people, that Leslie would come to me to talk. She knew I would call her eventually.

When I told her what Leslie had said, she cried some more and said she knew that she was O.K. She just missed her so much. We talked for a long time that afternoon and shared the wonder and awesomeness of how our God can bring all of us hope in any circumstance. We just need to be open to it, accept it, and share it with each other.

A Child Shall Lead

My prayer for you:

❀   ❀   ❀

THEN THE EYES OF THE BLIND BE OPENED AND THE EARS OF THE DEAF UNSTOPPED. THEN WILL THE LAME LEAP LIKE A DEER, AND THE MUTE TONGUE SHOUT FOR JOY.

LIFE IS FULL OF TWISTS AND TURNS, UNEXPECTED HIGHS AND LOWS.

HEAVENLY FATHER, I ASK THAT YOU SURROUND ALL OF YOUR CHILDREN, YOUNG AND OLD, WITH YOUR PRESENCE SO THAT WE WILL FEEL YOUR LOVE NO MATTER WHAT CIRCUMSTANCE WE FIND OURSELVES IN. I ASK THAT YOU OPEN OUR HEARTS TO YOU AND KEEP OUR EYES LIFTED SO THAT WE CAN SEE THE TRUTH AND BEAUTY YOU SO GRACIOUSLY PROVIDE TO US EACH DAY.

IN YOUR NAME I PRAY THESE THINGS. AMEN.

CHAPTER EIGHT
Peace

❋   ❋   ❋

"And the peace of God, which transcends all understanding, will guard your hearts and your minds in Christ Jesus." Philippians 4:7

One month after Leslie died, I was sitting alone in my office, which was a rarity as I shared that space with four other staff members. My back was to the door and I was crying, my head in my hands, mourning the death of this precious student who meant so much to me.

Suddenly, I was keenly aware of another presence in the room. The hairs stood up on my arms and I got very quiet. I had not heard the door opening nor the footsteps that had come closer, stopping behind me.

I turned slowly as I wiped the tears that had fallen from my eyes and were clinging to my cheeks. I expected to see a nurse or another staff member who needed my services for a patient. That's not who I saw at all.

Standing before me in silence with eyes wide open and filled with sorrow stood Leslie's best friend. He looked at me pleadingly as I stood to embrace him. He couldn't speak. I reached for him and pulled him tight to comfort him while he sobbed.

Tears flowed from both us as we cried for the loss of our friend. I was trying to pull myself together, as we weren't supposed to "break down and cry" in front of our patients. We weren't supposed to "hug" them tightly either.

We were "supposed" to hold it together, be "professional," "not cross emotional boundaries" and "cry when we were alone, somewhere out of sight." Sure, this all sounds good in theory, and during training and most of the time, it's possible to carry out these "expectations"; however, at this particular moment, it was not.

After a few minutes, he pulled away, looking up at me brokenly, and asked, "Will you please tell me what happened? No one will talk to me. They're avoiding me like it's a secret and too painful to talk about. They are acting like I don't know, but I do. I do know! Leslie died and I want to know every detail of what happened. Please," he begged. "Please tell me her story."

You see, he needed to know and was desperate to find out because he too had cystic fibrosis. His reality had just slapped him in the face, and he needed to be prepared.

Thoughts were flying through my brain: *What are you doing here?...What! Are you kidding me?...Why hasn't anyone told you?...Why didn't your mom tell you?...That seems unreal!...This is ridiculous!...I am a teacher, I'm not a therapist!...I am not the one who is supposed to be debriefing a grief situation...I don't know how to do this...How am I going to do this?...Oh, Lord, please help me do this!*

Chapter Eight: Peace

After my quick minute-long freakout, I took a deep breath and realized that, of course, I was going to be the one to tell him. I was going to tell him because I understood that he needed the truth. He needed that peace from anxiety that only God's peace can bring.

I knew God's presence was with Leslie, and as a witness to her passing, it was going to be my privilege to be able to share her story with him. He was already a believer, and in the past, during previous hospital stays, he had shared his walk with Jesus with me.

I decided I would be as open and honest as I knew how, and that I would answer any question he threw at me.

"What do you want to know?" I said softly as we both took a seat in my office. I brought the box of tissue from my desk over to the table and sat it between us.

"Did it hurt?" he asked. "Does it hurt when you die?"

Well, I thought, *Here we go...how am I supposed to answer that? Maybe I'm not going to do so well at this after all.* Then I reflected back to those last few hours in the hospital room where family and friends surrounded Leslie, and I said with honesty, "No, I don't believe it did."

I continued, "Leslie looked like she was taking a nap. She had her eyes closed and looked like she was at peace. Her breathing looked effortless [which is a big deal when you have CF]. She was hooked up to the 'pump' so the nurses and doctors could monitor her heart rate and oxygen levels and give her medication through her IV. She had her family in the room taking turns talking to her the entire time. I even had a chance to sit on her bed and talk with her a little bit."

"Were you there?" he asked in earnest. "Were you in the room?"

"Yes," I stated. "I was in the room, too."

"No!" he exclaimed with much more conviction. "I mean, were you in the room when she died?" I covered his hand with mine and looked him in the eye with tenderness as I softly said, "Yes, I was there when she died. I was there the entire time, through the whole process."

It was as if he had breathed a huge sigh of relief when he heard those words. He stared at the floor for a moment and then said, "I don't want to die alone."

His lip started to quiver and I said, "Sweetheart, I'm sure your mom and dad will be by your side. I'm sure you won't be alone." He looked at me square in the eye and said nothing, not sure whether to believe me. I could tell he was thinking that there were many days that he was in the hospital alone, where he didn't have anyone visiting him. How could I guarantee that his mom and dad would actually be there by his side? I couldn't make that promise.

Then he whispered, "You were there with Leslie when she died. Will you be with me when I die, too?" Uh, oh, here we go again, another "rule" we aren't supposed to break: *Never make promises that you absolutely can't keep.*

How can I say yes when I have no idea when his death might occur? So again, with honesty I said, "I don't know when you are going to die. I hope that it is a very long time from now. What I do know is this, if you are here in the hospital and I am here in the hospital *and* you are dying, I will do everything in my power to be in your presence when your time has come."

Chapter Eight: Peace

"What if I'm in pain?" he said, this fear obviously pressing on his mind. I told him, "Our doctors aren't going to let you be in pain. They check on you constantly and know what to look for even when you can't talk. They won't let you be in any pain." I was confident in our team and knew firsthand that they went above and beyond for every one of our kids, yet my heart pounded out of my chest because I didn't *really* know if the kids were in pain or not. I couldn't feel what they were feeling. I could only guess that what the doctors did, worked. I could only rely on my faith and my prayers and would continue to lift up my worries and inabilities to God, as I did know He could take care of it all. Those words seemed to ease his fears somewhat. He sat back in his chair and said solemnly, "O.K., now I'm ready to hear the whole story about Leslie. Tell me everything and start from the beginning."

Surprisingly, the words poured out of me without effort. I answered his questions in the order in which he asked. Afterwards, we shared memories and funny stories about her personality. Gratefully, we shared moments of laughter intermittently dispersed amongst our tears.

He reminisced about the times they had spent together as kids and how they would sneak to see each other in the nurse's office at school during treatments, knowing they were supposed to keep their distance due to the risk of causing each other an infection.

When he felt as though he had heard enough of the details, he stopped, looked at me and said, "They are going to admit me today. My lungs aren't getting any better and my weight is down."

Am I in a time warp? What is going on? I swallowed hard and forced a smile that I hoped he would see as genuine, while saying, "O.K. then, let's get your schedule in place so you can get that school work tackled while you are here." Smiling back, he nodded and said, "O.K., we'll start tomorrow. They're putting me in the room across the hall and my mom is bringing my books this afternoon."

I walked him to the classroom door. Feeling a sense of foreboding that I could not shake, I watched him walk across the hall to his room.

30 days later

The days passed and turned into a month. I thought the pattern seemed too familiar. His lungs weren't healing and his weight was decreasing. He wasn't eating. He wasn't spending much time out of his room.

School went from classroom instruction to bedside lessons. I walked onto the floor one morning and was setting up my classroom for that day's lessons, gathering materials for the day, when a nurse came in and asked me if I had heard the news? News? What news? No, I hadn't heard any news. She told me that my student was downstairs in the Intensive Care Unit and things didn't look so good. Things had changed overnight, his health declining so quickly that they transferred him into the ICU.

Was his family with him? Nobody seemed to know. I tripped over chairs as I ran towards the stairwell. Panicked, I raced down four flights of stairs, holding onto the rail so I wouldn't go head first in a tumble. I prayed that his mom, dad, sister, *someone* who loved him was there so

Chapter Eight: Peace

he wouldn't be alone. I prayed that I'd get there in time, because I knew his greatest fear was that of dying alone.

When I made it to the fourth floor, I frantically searched the board, looking for his initials to indicate which room they had him in. I passed the waiting room and out of the corner of my eye, I saw them all.

His mom, dad, sister, friends from his church, aunts and uncles; they were all there waiting. My knees were weak and I almost fell to the floor in gratitude. He wouldn't be alone. He would not die alone.

I went over to his mom who was sitting in a chair next to the window. I knelt beside her, taking her hands in mine. "What can I do?" I asked. "How can I help you right now?" She looked at me and smiled. She said calmly, "Go and be with him. He's been asking for you."

I was suddenly scared. I mean, what if he died and I was in there alone? I didn't want that for his parents and family. I wanted them to be there with him; that's who mattered, not me. She must have seen my thoughts on my face, and she nudged me, saying, "Go, it will be O.K. I'll be there soon enough." She seemed so at peace, so sure. That calmed me somehow, so I stood, turned, walked out of the waiting room and headed down the hall to say my final goodbyes.

When I got into his room it was quiet, just the steady beeping of the machines monitoring his body's report. I looked at him lying there, as if he was taking a nap. At peace. Breathing as if it wasn't a chore. I sat on his bed and talked to him, telling him that his entire family was down the hall waiting to come see him. I thanked him for being the person he was and the friend to all those whom he met.

I asked him to tell Leslie hello, as I knew she'd be there waiting to show him the way. I held his hand and kissed his forehead, then headed out the door.

I went back to the waiting room and hugged his mom tightly. I thanked her for sharing her son with me. She smiled and walked away. The rest of the family followed. This time, the immediate family members were the only ones in the room when the passing occurred.

I was in the hallway standing outside the door looking in, my presence there because I had "promised" that if I could, I'd be there when he died.

I saw his mom crawl up into the bed next to him, rocking him and telling him it was O.K. to let go. She held him while he took his final breath. I don't believe he was in any pain, and I know he wasn't alone.

Peace:
So many of us think we have to have all of the answers to be considered "wise" or smart. Anxiety and anger ensues when we feel we can't answer questions correctly. Schools teach us that we must always be "right" and that "wrong" is a failure.

Reality is that we don't need all of the answers if we embrace our gifts and look to others to share their gifts with us. Christian ministry is a team effort, and we all have differing gifts that were given to us at birth.

What does the word "gift" represent to you? I visualize something fun, something exciting, unknown and special. People who care, who want us to know that we have meaning in their life, give gifts to us.

God cares enough about us that He gave us something truly special, something designed just for us, something unique, something to be cultured. We should embrace these gifts and use them wholeheartedly to further God's Kingdom.

Often it takes time to understand what your gift actually is and to use it accordingly. Sometimes we ignore our gifts, or rather put them away for another time when it is more convenient to use, or when we feel we have more time to enjoy them.

When we "shelve" our gifts, we are not the only ones missing their value. We risk relationships and experiences that could bring our friends, family and acquaintances peace, love and positive change. When we share our gifts with others, we automatically get more in return.

Now I know what some of you are thinking: *"I don't have the energy to share my gifts all the time!"* We allow our busy schedules or life's annoyances to get in our way.

I get it. I have done the same thing. In all honesty, there have been times where I have purposely "shelved" my gift because I was too emotionally stretched. I was tired of sharing, I wasn't feeling that "return." I felt empty, tired. I felt alone.

But here is the important part, where the peace comes into play. I've learned that you are actually never alone. In Matthew 11:28, Jesus tells us these words, *"Come to me, all you who are weary and burdened, and I will give you rest. Take My yoke upon you and learn from Me, for I am gentle and humble in heart, and you will find rest for your souls. For My yoke is easy and My burden is light."*

This doesn't mean that you won't have struggles or burdens throughout your life. However, if you lift them up to be carried by Jesus, your load will lighten and you will begin to really feel His love, healing and peace.

All you have to do is ask and believe that He is walking next to you, listening. He cries with you, like a friend. He smiles broadly at your accomplishments, like a friend. His love will carry you through it.

Lean on Him. Go ahead, He can take it! The more you lean on Him, the more peace you will find.

> **My prayer for you:**
>
> ❊ ❊ ❊
>
> AND THE PEACE OF GOD, WHICH TRANSCENDS ALL UNDERSTANDING, WILL GUARD YOUR HEARTS AND YOUR MINDS IN CHRIST JESUS.
>
> WE ARE CREATED INDIVIDUALLY, WITH HEARTS THAT FEEL EMOTIONS AT ALL LEVELS. AS WE INTERSECT IN ONE ANOTHER'S LIVES, WE MAY FIND OURSELVES SHARING MUTUAL PAIN.
>
> DEAR GOD, I ASK THAT IN TIMES WHEN ALL OF US SEEM TO BE FUMBLING THROUGH SHARED SADNESS, THAT YOU REST YOUR HANDS ON US SO THAT WE CAN REMAIN SAFE, RESTORED AND TENDED TO. THANK YOU FOR ALLOWING US TO EXPERIENCE LIFE AND DEATH SO THAT WE CAN OFFER SUPPORT TO OTHERS IN THEIR HOURS OF DARKNESS.
>
> THESE THINGS I ASK IN YOUR NAME. AMEN.

CHAPTER NINE
Fluff
❃   ❃   ❃

"But He said to me, 'My grace is sufficient for you, for my power is made perfect in weakness.' Therefore I will boast all the more gladly about my weakness, so that Christ's power may rest on me. That is why, for Christ's sake, I delight in weaknesses, in insults, in hardships, in persecutions, in difficulties. For when I am weak, then I am strong." 2 Corinthians 12:9-11

A long time ago, while attending a party, someone asked me what I did for my work. I responded with, "I am a teacher." He asked me what I taught and I told him that I was a special education teacher and taught kids from kindergarten through eighth grade.

The next comment out of his mouth stunned me.

His eyes rolled a little and a smirk crossed his face as he said in a condescending tone, "Oh, *special ed*. You're not a *real* teacher, you just play games and keep *those* kids entertained so their parents can have a break. Isn't what you do just called 'fluff'?"

I was shocked. I didn't even know what to say to that. Fury swelled inside of me. His insult made my heart break for the students he so quickly and carelessly disregarded.

For days I pondered his comment, wondering how I could have responded if I had been able to speak.

Here is what I came up with.

Have you ever been to the grocery store and stood in the peanut butter aisle, contemplating crunchy or smooth? There are so many brands and choices. Heck, you can even get peanut butter and jelly swirled together if you don't want to buy two individual jars for your sandwich.

On this same set of shelves, you might see something called Nutella—a delicious hazelnut chocolate treat that tastes more like dessert than a sandwich spread. If you look further, you may even find something called "marshmallow creme," or "Fluff" for short.

I *love* Fluff!

You can do so many things with this stuff. You can make peanut butter Fluff sandwiches, also known as the "Fluffernutter." You can use it to make chocolate fudge. You can melt it and use it as an ice cream topping. You can rim a martini glass with it and pour crushed candies on top to make your drink look dazzling. Also, you can eat it straight from the jar, because it tastes just like a melted marshmallow on a s'more.

Did I mention that I love Fluff?

Open a jar of it and take a peek inside. It is actually a beautiful sight. It is a pure shade of white and glistens with a flawless presence. Smooth, shiny, light and fun.

I smile every time, no matter how many jars I've eaten.

Chapter Nine: Fluff

When you stick your spoon or knife into the jar for the first time, it bounces right back, covering up the indentation that you have just created.

Making a sandwich looks easy enough. Just scoop out some Fluff and spread it on your bread. Add peanut butter and you have a quick delicious snack.

However, this is not what happens.

Fluff is deceiving.

Fluff becomes sticky when you spread it onto your bread. Careful, you don't want to get any on your fingers, as this stuff is hard to get off.

It seems to multiply, and the next thing you know, everything you've touched has evidence of Fluff.

Fluff is messy! Before you know it, it is all over your knife, your hands, your face and on your bread. What started out as a simple task has pretty quickly become more complicated. Sounds similar to teaching: all kinds of teaching, but especially teaching within the realm of special education You want to compare teaching kids with special needs with Fluff? Let's do it!

When I look at my students, I see resilience. Just like the jar of Fluff when the first knife makes an indentation into its core. The Fluff bounces back, covering up the empty space.

How many of these kids have had their "core" or heart broken with harsh words or judgments? I see it in the school halls as kids pass from class to class. I watch during lunchtime, where chatter and excitement are evident everywhere except the table where my students sit.

How many of these children were considered less worthy of a real education or a "real" teacher simply based on a title or a category?

Does this break them? Not at first. They cover it up and carry on, figuring out ways to adapt in order to survive.

Some people want these kids to be "simple" or "easy," but they're not.

They are innocent and pure on the outside, but when you start digging deeper you find that their needs and abilities may get messy, sticky and difficult to let go.

Some may say that the benefit of Fluff is not worth the fight. Really?

God created us all with limitations; some are just more apparent than others. He did this on purpose, with a reason behind each individual thorn. Some of our thorns are visible: maybe our limbs don't work properly or our brains have differing connections. Some thorns are transparent and only recognizable through our actions and our words.

Regardless of what our limitations are, He designed them for us to be able to recognize them and embrace them. We need them in order to rely on Him for our complete strength.

If we were made without weakness, we would become arrogant or full of pride—both weaknesses on their own. Our reliance on God would be vulnerable and our lives would become empty.

When I interact with my students, their outward disabilities disappear and I am able to see and focus on their souls, the souls of beautiful human beings.

I watch as acceptance, resolve and determination unfold. I see forgiveness play out through grace. I learn from these

Chapter Nine: Fluff

children. They humble me with their knowledge. They witness to me through their weakness.

So my friend, you asked me if what I did was Fluff. My answer to you is "yes." What I do is just like Fluff! I love that stuff... Fluff. It makes me smile—every... single ... time.

My prayer for you:

❋ ❋ ❋

BUT HE SAID TO ME, 'MY GRACE IS SUFFICIENT FOR YOU, FOR MY POWER IS MADE PERFECT IN WEAKNESS.' THEREFORE I WILL BOAST ALL THE MORE GLADLY ABOUT MY WEAKNESS, SO THAT CHRIST'S POWER MAY REST ON ME. THAT IS WHY, FOR CHRIST'S SAKE, I DELIGHT IN WEAKNESSES, IN INSULTS, IN HARDSHIPS, IN PERSECUTIONS, IN DIFFICULTIES. FOR WHEN I AM WEAK, THEN I AM STRONG.

DEAR HEAVENLY FATHER, SOMETIMES OUR LIVES GET STICKY AND COMPLICATED AND HARD FOR US TO HANDLE.

I ASK FOR YOUR HAND TO GUIDE US IN THESE MOMENTS. TAKE OUR HANDS INTO YOURS AND SHOW US HOW TO CLEAN UP THE MESS THAT WE CAN FEEL BUT MAY NOT ALWAYS SEE. HELP US TO USE WORDS THAT ARE GENTLE SO THAT HURTFUL COMMENTS NO LONGER EXIST IN OUR VOCABULARY. SHOW US HOW TO LIVE WITH LOVE AND GRACE SO THAT WE CAN BE AN EXAMPLE TO OTHERS THAT COME INTO OUR LIVES.

THESE THINGS I ASK IN YOUR NAME. AMEN.

CHAPTER TEN
Slurpees and Other Simple Acts of Kindness
❊ ❊ ❊

"Share with God's people who are in need. Practice hospitality." Romans 12:13

We've all known a co-worker, friend or family member who has been in need at some point over the course of their lives. Often, we feel unprepared as to the best way to help them. What should we say? What should we not say? What should we do? What if we do the wrong thing?

My friends and I joke that when someone is in need and we don't know what to do, we show up with a "crisis chicken." Sometimes, this is literally a baked chicken with some sides, sometimes it is a plate of homemade cookies, and sometimes it's a simple bag of chips and some salsa.

The point is that it actually doesn't matter what you show up *with*. The point is to just show up.

The friendly reception and treatment of guests or strangers is the definition of hospitality. Hospitality can happen anywhere and in any way.

A Child Shall Lead

One example of hospitality provided by a complete stranger to my sister and me happened in a hospital waiting room. Our mom was having surgery in a large, sterile hospital that, while filled with talented doctors and staff, lacked any kind of environmental stimuli to create comfort during a stay.

My sister and I sat in the waiting room on hard metal chairs. Along with strangers, we sat quietly staring at a white wall and a TV, which was tuned into the only channel that was visible through intermittent static. Those who wanted to read could choose from the multitude of pamphlets displayed on the one bulletin board by the door. The pamphlets contained exciting information on various medical conditions that one could look forward to if his or her body decided to betray itself.

After taking in all that the room had to offer, I decided to search for a gift store so I could bring back some "real reading material" for my sister and me to peruse. It took me a while to find this gift shop. As I mentioned, the hospital lacked helpful environmental stimuli, including informative signage.

Once I returned, I checked in with my sister to see if there had been any news or changes during my absence. She told me there hadn't been, and we sat and read while we continued our wait.

After a couple more hours passed, we were thirsty and uncomfortable from sitting for so long. We didn't want to go to the cafeteria. For one, we didn't know where it was and more importantly, we didn't want to leave in case the doctors came in to share an update on our mom.

Chapter Ten: Slurpees and Other Simple Acts of Kindness

We were beginning to feel anxious, thinking that a longer-than-expected surgery surely meant there was a bigger problem to face. Neither of us was comfortable leaving, so we continued to stay in our "waiting space."

As if on cue, in walked a volunteer. She greeted us with a soft hello as she wheeled in a cart, which carried coffee, hot water, tea bags and hot chocolate packets. She set the drinks and cups on one of the counter tops and left us with napkins and a tray of cookies as well. Suddenly, this room was transformed.

I felt my heart open and the stress on my shoulders melt away. Along with that, I somehow felt a new sense of relief. It was almost silly how this small offer of hospitality, provided by a complete stranger, brought gentleness and light into a sterile, anxiety-filled room.

Each of us walked to the counter and got a beverage and a cookie. Communication began to unfold. We started to talk to one another, asking about reasons for being there. This time of fellowship and sharing eased most of our fears and provided a sense of community during the remainder of our stay.

If a stranger can provide hospitality that creates a lasting and warm memory, imagine what kind of impact your hospitality could create with your family and friends.

When my father died, I was 26 years old. We were on a family vacation at the beach where we had been going since I was a kid. We were there with several other families I had known since birth. These were my father's best friends—people who, in reality, were more like family.

During the days, we all were able to do our own thing. Most of us swam, laid in the sun and took walks to gather shells. We'd run in and out of the beach house to bring sandwiches or drinks down to the others on the sand. Tradition was that around 4 p.m., we all had to be showered and ready for the family cocktail hour and dinner. Dinners rotated by family and often included a theme.

Rotating 10 to 12 people through the showers was no easy feat. There was a delicate dance of who should go in what order, as we all wanted a least a little hot water to bathe.

This particular day, as I was about last in line, I asked my mom to let my dad go before me, as I wanted him to have any hot water that might be remaining. My dad had gone to their room to rest until it was his turn for the shower. When my mom went to wake him, she found him unresponsive. Her screams alerted the rest of us that something was dreadfully wrong.

I jumped up and ran into their room, where I saw my dad on the bed looking like he was asleep, yet not. I began to shake him and scream out his name. No response. I struggled to drag his lifeless body to the floor where I began to administer CPR. Chest compressions, breaths and prayers in a frantically sustained rhythm. Everyone started gathering around while we waited for the ambulance to arrive. More chest compressions, more breaths, more prayers. Nothing.

The paramedics arrived and took him to the nearest hospital, which was about 45 minutes away. We all jumped into our cars and started the procession behind the ambulance. I was the last to arrive, as I had to stay back and provide

Chapter Ten: Slurpees and Other Simple Acts of Kindness

the police with a report. When I walked into the emergency room, I saw the rest of my family and friends gathered together. They had placed us in a private room where we would wait for our final answer.

I looked out the window of the room where we all stood, and I saw two medical staff approaching the door. They hesitated before entering and took a deep breath. It was at that moment that I knew. My father had been pronounced dead on arrival. They explained that they had continued life-saving efforts in the ambulance ride, to no avail.

My mom fell into the arms of her friend, my sister almost fainted and I just stared in disbelief. These two doctors stayed in that room and offered hospitality to us in our time of need. Eventually, they asked if we wanted some time alone with my dad. They took the time to explain what they had done, what my dad would look like and that we could stay as long as we wanted. Hospitality in this sense was provided with gentleness and through time.

After my dad's funeral, there were days that were lonely and long as we all grieved in our own ways, but acts of hospitality removed some of that isolation and sadness. People who offer hospitality are willingly sharing in your time of need.

To this day, I am still humbled by those "simple" acts of kindness. There was a knock at our back door one day, and there stood a friend holding three large Slurpees. I was so happy! These were drinks we loved as kids, and we would ask special permission so that we could ride our bikes down to the 7-11 to get one.

After he sat the drinks down on the table, I gave him a huge hug and thanked him for his kindness. He said it was "nothing," and that he didn't really know what to do to make us feel better. He said that he was driving by the 7-11 and figured a Slurpee couldn't hurt. We took our drinks into the living room and told stories of our childhood favorite foods and laughed all the way to that last sip.

It was the mix of nostalgia, the ability to laugh when sad and the fact that even though he admittedly stated he didn't know what to do, he showed up anyway, that meant the world.

Food, especially food that we deem "comfort food," provides a sense of relief and order to our lives. It is meant to be unpretentious, sentimental and make us feel good.

After my dad died, we didn't gather at the beach for quite a few years, losing the tradition that had been built since childhood. This seemed like a different kind of loss to me. I moved across the country, starting a life with people who never knew my dad, which only added to the isolation I felt each year on the anniversary of his death.

One of my new friends asked me about my family while we were having lunch. As it ended up, we had both lost a parent and were able to share our memories to one another. One of the things I told her was that every year, on the anniversary of my dad's death, I always drink a beer and eat something that he really liked as my way to toast his memory.

A year later, I received a message from this friend asking me if I was out having a beer and toasting my dad. This message came on the anniversary of his death. The fact that

Chapter Ten: Slurpees and Other Simple Acts of Kindness

she remembered this and took the time to send this note touched my heart greatly. She extended a simple hospitality that I will carry forever.

Sometimes, things come full circle. Several years ago, our beach family decided it was time to reunite again. By now, we had all spread out from the West Coast to the Southeast. It took one phone call, and we were all set to meet again at the beach that summer. We screeched and squealed with excitement as we set into motion our traditions from days past.

During the last night's dinner, my dad's best friend stood to give a toast. He toasted all of us and shared that it had been too long in between trips. He toasted the week as he laughed and recapped the events that took place. Then he raised his glass and started to cry. His tears caught in his throat as he started to speak. He toasted his friend, my dad, telling us that he was missed greatly, that he'll never be forgotten and that his spirit will forever be among us. Semper Fi, dear friend, Semper Fi.

Opportunities to extend hospitality present themselves everyday. Our calling is to respond to these when presented. Remember, even what we consider a small act of kindness may have a lasting impact on the person's heart. Your acts are powerful and hold great meaning. Set positive change in motion. Do what your heart leads you to do. Live out your faith. Now is the time.

Let's live out our faith by being hospitable to others.

My prayer for you:

❋ ❋ ❋

SHARE WITH GOD'S PEOPLE WHO ARE IN NEED. PRACTICE HOSPITALITY.

SIMPLE ACTS OF KINDNESS. IF WE ALL DID JUST ONE OF THESE A DAY, CAN YOU IMAGINE THE IMPACT IT WOULD HAVE ON OUR WORLD? HOSPITALITY CAN HEAL HEARTS.

GOD, TODAY I ASK THAT YOU INSTILL IN US THE DESIRE TO REACH OUT TO OTHERS, ESPECIALLY WHEN WE KNOW THEY ARE IN PAIN. HELP US TO JUST SHOW UP, REGARDLESS OF WHETHER OR NOT WE KNOW WHAT TO SAY OR DO. GIVE US THE COURAGE TO JUST SIT AND BE A FRIEND. I THANK YOU FOR BRINGING THOSE FRIENDS INTO MY LIFE DURING MY TIMES OF SADNESS. WE ARE ALL CAPABLE OF PROVIDING HOSPITALITY.

I LIFT THIS UP IN YOUR NAME, LORD. AMEN.

Chapter Eleven
Judgment
❊ ❊ ❊

"May the words of my mouth and the mediation of my heart be pleasing in your sight, O Lord, my Rock and my Redeemer."
Psalm 19:14

Would you change the way you lived if you knew that God was examining your every word, thought or action?

It's not an easy task, to speak or think without offering judgment. I'd like to think that most of the time, I act in a way that is respectable to myself, my family and most importantly, my God. But this simply is not the truth.

I have plenty of moments where my emotions take control of the situation and I find myself criticizing those around me. This is not how I want to be, and so I say to myself, *Change it!* Easier said than done. It's hard to take that step back and let the experience play out as if it were a movie being shown on a big screen with me as the observer, not the main character. This is especially the case when I'm tired, burned out from work or frustrated with life. It's something I work at every day.

A Child Shall Lead

It is important for us to step back and reserve judgment. We actually have no idea what is happening in the lives of others at any given moment. Sure, we like to think we know. After all, these people are our friends, our co-workers and people living in our community. We see them, we watch their behavior and understand their personalities. And, on some levels, we may have a general understanding. But really, it's what we don't see, what lies out of our line of vision, that may be the underlying force to all that exists on the surface.

Many years ago, I worked with a spunky little tweener who lived with a chronic illness. She spent a lot of her time with us in the hospital. She was an only child to a single mom. She wasn't raised with money and owned only a few items that she called her own. She never let on that she needed a thing, even though she was outspoken and feisty, all in a good way.

Her mom showed the burden of living a difficult life. She chose to display her feelings with art on her skin, which was revealed openly by her clothing. Her hair was tousled with a from-the-box blonde look. Without knowing her, you'd say she was "a little rough around the edges."

All this, coupled with the fact that she oftentimes wasn't at her daughter's side, made her an easy target for judgments. People would ask: "Where is she?" "Doesn't she care about her daughter?" "Have you *seen* the way she dresses?"

I heard these comments from people I worked with everyday—people that I liked and respected. I didn't want them to judge so harshly, yet could understand their concerns.

Chapter Eleven: Judgment

I tried to soften their approach by defending this mom. "Maybe she has to work during the day and can't be here," I'd say. "It's hot outside, maybe she likes to wear tank tops in the sun." Grasping at straws but having no real answers, I just wanted to lessen the impact the words might have on my student's ears.

The hospital stay continued, and a move to the Intensive Care Unit was needed. Here, my tweener was more isolated and the visits from her mom lessened. She was in a place medically where she wasn't going to survive. Can you imagine the words that circled around now?

At my visit one day, she asked if we could work on math. This was what she wanted to accomplish before she died. She wanted to make sure she learned all of the math lessons for her grade so she could say she completed something in its entirety.

We worked on math for days. During this time, I didn't see her mom. I wondered if she did visit at all and told myself she must be coming at night. Staff members were getting angry, as they didn't want this young girl to be alone during her last days on earth. I understood but knew there must be a reason for a mother to not be present at a time like this. We all tried to fill that void as sadness and confusion enveloped us. When I'd feel myself slipping into that harsh judgment zone, I reminded myself to pull back and wait, opening my mind to other possible options.

I tried to keep things light during our interactions. We worked on academics and also took pictures for keepsakes. We decorated her room, making it more "homelike," as this was her space for the rest of her time.

After her death, we got a notice of when the services would be held. Two of us decided to go to her funeral and celebration of life, as we had spent a lot of hospital time with this young lady. We wanted her mom to know that people from the hospital cared about her daughter and were there to support her, too.

We sat in a small room inside the funeral home, quietly staring at her casket up front. There weren't a lot of people there, her family and friend circle being small. I saw her mom, dressed in the best outfit she owned. She had washed and straightened her hair, but still had a look of great unease on her face. Caring for a chronically ill child and trying to work to make ends meet had etched deep lines into her skin. No one can truly understand that weight unless you've been there yourself.

The service was about to begin, and I watched as she walked toward me. I wondered where she was going, as she should have been taking her seat up front. She stopped and kneeled at my side, leaning her head to whisper something into my ear. She had a request.

"Will you stand up front and talk about Dee? I can't do it, and you know her the best out of everyone else here." Shock must have registered on my face as I looked into her eyes.

"Please," she whispered with desperation.

"Of course," I answered gently. "Just give me a minute to collect my thoughts."

I bent my head and frantically began to pray. *Oh, Lord, please help me! Help guide me today, filling my heart with the emotions You want portrayed to this family. Fill my*

Chapter Eleven: Judgment

mouth with the words that will help to ease their pain; words they need to hear so that their minds and hearts can heal and so that they can understand Your grace. Oh, and one more quick thing, please help me so I don't pass out, thank You! Amen. I rose and walked slowly to the front of the room. I stood next to the casket and looked down at my student. I smiled at my memories then looked out into the crowd.

To be honest with you, I can't remember anything that I said on that day. My prayers must have been answered, though, as afterwards, the family and few friends that were present came up to me with tears in their eyes. They thanked me for my words, which had eased some of their pain. They said they had never heard such warmth and love coming from someone else talking about their family and their lives. They surrounded me with emotional hugs.

I stood there afterwards, watching them all leave the room. I thanked God for His guidance and for allowing me to be His vessel on this day.

The after celebration was held at Dee's house. It was a small home on a dirt lot, located on the outskirts of town. Neighbors had dropped off some food and sodas, so we arranged them on the folding table out back. We gathered there to share stories and fellowship amongst strangers and friends.

Dee's mom had purchased a dozen pink balloons and asked us to write a note and tie it to the end. After we had secured our notes to our respective balloons, we gathered in a circle and said one final goodbye to a beautiful little girl. On the count of three, we raised our arms and let the wind carry our messages toward the cloud-filled sky.

I stepped away from the crowd for a moment so that I could soak in that special memory and sear it to my soul. My face was raised to the sun, eyes closed, while I reflected on the hospital stays and the harsh words that had been spoken there. I pictured the family pulling together in a time of unfathomable pain.

I sensed a presence near me and looked over to see Dee's mom standing at my side. She looked at me with purpose and said, "I know what everyone must have thought of me." I stayed quiet, sensing she needed to go on. "I know how they looked at me when I came to the floor. I could hear their whispers outside the room."

I started to speak, wanting her to know that they didn't mean what they had said. I didn't want her to be worrying about other people's comments today of all days. She stopped me, saying, "It's not the others I care about knowing the truth; it's *you*. I want you to know the reason why."

She went on to tell me that as the days became evident that Dee wasn't leaving the hospital, she became more and more scared and anxious. She wanted to make her baby girl better and was helpless in making that happen. I understood that and let her know everyone would understand that as well.

The intensity in her story increased as she continued. "I know people at the hospital thought I was an uncaring mom because they didn't see me in Dee's room. That's not the truth. I was there—every single day."

"You were?" I asked. She answered, "Yes! Every day I would drive 45 minutes one way from our house to the hospital. You know gas isn't cheap. I would go without food

Chapter Eleven: Judgment

some days just so I could come. And every single day, I would walk through the front doors and step onto the elevator. I would stand there and start to cry. I would weep for my daughter, as I knew she was upstairs needing me to be with her. I would stand there sobbing, as I couldn't control her fate. I wanted so badly to make her better.

"Then, I would turn around and walk back off the elevators, walk out of the hospital and just sit in my car."

My heart broke as I listened to her words. "Why?" I asked. "Why didn't you just come and let her see you cry?"

"Because, I didn't want her to think that her hope was gone. If she saw me crying so much she would know, she would know there was nothing else that could be done. I couldn't be the one to take her hope away." Her words had struck a chord.

She let me know that she was able to visit at night, coming into her room after Dee had fallen asleep. She was there, a mom caring for her child. She held her daughter while gently stroking her hair. She whispered loving words into her ears and told her how special she was. Tears continued to flow, but this way, when they fell, they went unseen and hope was still alive.

My prayer for you:

❋ ❋ ❋

MAY THE WORDS OF MY MOUTH AND THE MEDIATION OF MY HEART BE PLEASING IN YOUR SIGHT, O LORD, MY ROCK AND MY REDEEMER.

DEAR HEAVENLY FATHER, I THANK YOU FOR PROVIDING EACH OF US WITH THE ABILITY TO EXPRESS OURSELVES OPENLY. WORDS ARE SO POWERFUL, AND I PRAY THAT YOU WILL HELP ME TO USE MINE TO HEAL HEARTS RATHER THAN WOUND THEM. I LIFT UP TO YOU THOSE WHO HAVE BEEN WOUNDED BY HURTFUL COMMENTS SO THAT THEY MAY HEAL UNDER YOUR CARE.

I PRAY THIS IN YOUR NAME. AMEN.

CHAPTER TWELVE
Irony of It All
❊   ❊   ❊

"Come to Me, all you who are weary and burdened, and I will give you rest. Take My yoke upon you and learn from Me, for I am gentle and humble in heart and you will find rest for your souls." Matthew 11:28-29

She was too young to live alone in a house, yet not too young to take home the premature baby she had delivered that month. Hospital staff guided her every step, surrounding her like a soft feather bed envelops you when you are tired. Nurses showed her how to hold her fragile child and told her when the baby needed to eat. A social worker made sure that she herself knows where the cafeteria is located and provided her with money to pay for some food. What she didn't have was her own mother or the family she thought she did.

Word on the street was that she was abandoned and no one knew the identity of the baby's father. Staff assumed many things, questioning her relentlessly. She kept quiet, never disclosing the truth. Many staff became angry as their frustrations ran high. "We just want to protect her and help her child stay safe," they claimed.

No one was able to break her silence, which wasn't any wonder as I watched people treat her differently than the other moms on the floor. She recognized this as well and absorbed it all. Staff treated her like a child who was in their way and criticized her for not understanding what she should be doing. The other new moms were also staring and afraid, scared to leave the room for fear of what might happen when they are gone. Why were they judging this one just because she was young?

Does any mom know what to do when their fragile baby is in an incubator needing specialized care? They didn't seem to get angry with the "older moms," so why are they angry with the one who is young?

They didn't know her story. They didn't know her heart. But, in time, they would learn. We *all* would learn.

In the beginning, I told myself that I didn't want to get involved. I was angry at the social worker for referring me to this case. I had a range of emotions so thick that it took time to sort them through. My own judgments rose to the surface before I had even met this girl. *This is a young teen mom who made her choice, I don't have time to hand hold her through school. She'll take time away from other kids who really want to learn, and will it really matter in the end?* Then my pity party kicked in with, *Why do I always get the tough cases?*

I mumbled under my breath and begrudgingly walked down the several flights of stairs onto the unit where this young lady stayed. I was annoyed to say the least, only there

Chapter Twelve: Irony of It All

because I'd been asked, actually begged, to help. I stepped into her room and then we met.

I stared at her young face as we were introduced. She didn't look like she just had a baby. She was just a baby herself. She was shy and polite and asked me what I did at the hospital. I explained that I was a teacher and that I was there to help her stay in school so that one day, she'd be able to go to high school and graduate with her class.

I thought to myself, *When you graduate, your child will be 6 years old. I can barely comprehend what I'm seeing.*

As if she could read my mind, she said, "When I graduate, my baby will be 6 years old." I nodded my head and responded, "I like that you say *when* you graduate. That's the first step. We had better get started. We have a lot of ground to cover."

This young lady had not yet finished her 6th grade year. Her decision to stay in school was the catalyst in shaping the rest of her life.

We met together Monday through Friday each week for several months. We didn't jump right into academics, even though I was worried about how much we needed to cover. More important matters were at hand. We needed to build our rapport while weaving in a solid foundation of trust. Trust was something she knew little about.

Our days were both interesting and exhausting. She came to the classroom with her notebooks and assignments each day. She was always on time and willing to learn. She was thirsty for knowledge and I saw her childlike wonder and innocence emerge. She had a strong spirit. She was a survivor.

She also came with questions. Questions that I didn't want to have to answer. Questions that when answered could take us both to a place of no return.

Her questions started out simple. "Are you from Idaho? What is your favorite color? Why did you want to be a teacher?" Those were easy to answer, and I would ask her some of the same in return. She liked that; she felt like it was a fun get-to-know-you game. Each session started with a conversation and moved into a lesson of academics. This young lady was articulate and bright. She had potential that had not yet been cultivated.

After each session, I would walk her back to the floor where her baby stayed. I dropped her off in the waiting area each time with the plan for our next session. It was strange, in a way. She was happy and driven in school, yet as we approached the area where her baby stayed, she became withdrawn and silent, never inviting me in.

I realized that I had never met her child.

Every day, I would get a call after school and the staff would ask, "Well, did she tell you who the father of the baby is?" I would answer them the same way each time: "No, I haven't asked. When she is ready to talk about that, she will. I think you need to leave her alone!" I was thinking they needed to leave me alone, too.

It wasn't long before I learned that she loved to read, as she found it provided her with information. She told me that one day, she wanted to go to college. She wanted to become a lawyer so that she could help people who were in need. This was fantastic as now we had a long-term goal to work toward.

Chapter Twelve: Irony of It All

As our weeks passed, her questions became more complex. She wanted cultural expectations explained, religious myths and beliefs separated, and the human body explained. These questions I could handle, as they all had factual answers that could be supported with data and documents.

Next came the questions that I knew would bring us into new territory. She knew her questions were ones that I might not answer. She also knew she had nothing to lose.

She wanted to know when I had sex for the first time. When she asked me this, she stared me right in the eyes. At first, I thought she was testing me to see if I'd answer any question she'd throw out. I then realized that she was serious and needed to know the truth. I thought about making something up as she would have never known, but again, realized she *needed* to know the truth. The adults in her life had never been honest with her and I wasn't going to be like them. I told her my answer and she sat in silence for a while, thinking. Next, she wanted to know who it was that had taken my virginity and if I had actually loved that person.

We were treading in very fragile waters now. I sensed where she was going with her questioning and felt that she was almost ready to disclose what had happened to her. My stomach started to ache and my heart was pounding. If she did tell me how she got pregnant and who the father was, I would need to let the healthcare team know immediately. At the same time, I was filled with gratitude that this young lady might want to share with me deeper levels of her story.

A Child Shall Lead

I gently asked her the same question in return. After all, this was our pattern from day one. She looked at me and said, "I want to tell you, but I can't." I stayed silent, hoping she would continue. She went on to say that she knew everyone was asking whom the father of her baby was. She knew what they thought had happened but she wanted me to know the truth. I thanked her for giving me her trust and explained the concern of the staff. She understood, yet her silence ensued for another day.

Eventually, her story began to unfold. She told me that in the beginning, she didn't even know she was pregnant; she thought she was just getting fat from eating too much junk food. She didn't like that idea, as she had always been thin (and happy to be so). It was her older sister who told her she was pregnant and confirmed it with several pregnancy tests from the local drugstore. Her first response was fear of telling her mom. That quickly switched to concern over not fitting into her clothes. She actually waited several months before revealing the news to her mom. She had been able to hide her weight gain with baggy sweaters.

I asked about school and if anyone there had noticed. She said that she was only really able to go the first semester. Once she became pregnant, her morning sickness was too much for her to attend. She tried to go intermittently, but that didn't last very long.

"Did the school try to help?" I asked. She shook her head no with sadness. She wanted someone to pay attention. She wanted someone to help. Her older sister tried her best, yet she had a baby herself. Her mother was absent for days

Chapter Twelve: Irony of It All

and sometimes weeks at a time. This young lady was on her own.

She admitted she was scared but acted as if she weren't. She told me older boys were always around and slipped that she might have tried a beer once in a while.

I asked if her sister or those older boys were in school. She told me her sister attended an alternative school. The older boys had dropped out and she claimed they all had jobs. Her stories didn't always match up, so I tactfully pried while trying to extrapolate the truth. At times, she picked up on my line of questioning and slowly revealed more pieces to her life.

She jumped to the point where she actually had her baby, still silent about how she had gotten this far. The day she went into labor, she thought she was sick. Her stomach was hurting badly and she didn't know why. She had no prenatal care and there wasn't anyone in her life to share with her what to expect. Luckily, she was at her cousin's house and let her know she was in pain. Just a teen herself, her cousin's advice was to lie down and try to take a nap. Maybe this would help her stomachache go away.

Several hours later, she realized she might be having her baby. Her water had broken, but she thought she had urinated on herself. She told her cousin and they tried calling her mom. No answer. They finally reached the girl's aunt, who let them know she was on her way home. Her aunt drove her to the hospital, where this little girl was left to have her baby alone. She had so many questions but no one to address them or any of her needs. All were too busy attending to her baby, who needed critical care for a premature birth.

After the delivery, her own mother came to pay her a visit. There were no flowers or cards of congratulations, but rather a threat to remain silent on how she came to have a child. As quickly as she arrived, she turned and left, again deserting her daughter.

I stared at her in disbelief. Who does this to their child? My heart broke inside, wanting to take away this young girl's fear and pain. It was at that moment that I deliberately asked, "What about the baby's dad? Was he there with you?" She looked at me trying to decide if the time had come. She told me that he was not there, but that he knew. Alone, scared, and trying to act grown up, she said she liked the fact that she had something to call her own, something to care for, to call family...something she loved and hated at the same time.

Breakthrough.

The next week of class time involved no discussion about her pregnancy, baby or the father. The focus was academics and talk of returning to school. Her goal was to get back as soon as the doctors let her take her baby home. What she didn't understand was the doctors and social service agencies needed to find out where that "home" was going to be. Would they separate the two or allow them to remain together? In the interim, she stayed with her cousin and aunt, as her mom had made a choice to disappear.

There were a few sessions when her cousin came to school with us. I observed this 16-year-old watching her; wishing she could trade places with a 13-year-old child

Chapter Twelve: Irony of It All

mother imagining that a baby could also help her to escape her own scattered life. I couldn't help but wonder what are we doing? Are we creating a façade that from the outside looks safe, fun and secure? Or, are we making a difference, planting those seeds that will help turn something unfathomable into some sort of goodness?

The day came when I found out the truth. Finally, disclosure. This day took months of trust building to create. Here we sat, the two of us around a table in a small room filled with books and materials. As I sorted through her homework papers, I noticed a printed picture of a young man's face.

"Who is this?" I asked. Without hesitation she answered, "That is my boyfriend." Boyfriend? She had never mentioned a boyfriend before. I took the picture and asked her to tell me about him.

She giggled at first, as if this were her first crush. Then in all seriousness, she looked at me and said, "*He* is the father of my baby." I looked back at the picture and asked his age. Knowing this was the moment in time that would change the course of her life, she hesitated and then told me the truth, her story. Her burden had lifted slightly, and mine had increased in size.

It was difficult to absorb the reality of what I heard. I didn't know what to do with her information. I knew what I was legally obligated to do, but I didn't want to betray this young girl's trust. She shared her secret with *me* because she didn't want the others to know.

I had to explain to her what my obligations were and why. I wanted her to know that by me telling the others, it was not an act of betrayal toward her. Instead, it was a chance for the staff to do what it could to take care of her and her baby. But I knew that she wrestled with choices and loyalties and had no idea whom she could trust with her story without fear of shame creeping in.

As we worked through the intricacy of her disclosure, more questions emerged. She was no longer careful and began blurting out her requests boldly. Her fear presented itself in survival tactics that were pushing my very own buttons with force. She asked me if I had kids, and when I answered "no" she demanded to know why. She asked if I had ever *wanted* to be a mom, resentful of the fact that she was one so young. She asked me where I lived, if I had a boyfriend, asked about my friends, and what I did when I wasn't at work.

Anger, envy and despair were all we could see in front of us, the two of us sharing those emotions wrapped together, suspended in time. Here sat a child who didn't want to be a mom, angry at her life. Here sat a woman who wanted more than anything to become a mom, angry at her life.

Acceptance—difficult at times, yet wonderfully freeing when accomplished. This young teen mom helped me come to accept my own circumstances in life, and I'd like to think I helped her do the same. I knew there had been a shift in thought, as on this day, she asked me a monumental question.

"Would you like to come and meet my baby?" she said softly. The answer to this one came easily. "Of course!" I said with a genuine smile in my heart. We walked together into her room, and she offered her child up to me to hold.

I held that baby close, feeling warmth as our burdens released. She softly spoke the words, "You know, my baby has my eyes, and my feet, and my smile, and..."

She stood against the window where sunrays broke through the clouds. I watched this young woman's heart fill with peace, while simultaneously, mine filled, too. What a journey this young lady had traveled. Her load had been heavy and her burden great, yet she continued forward. Along her winding road, she learned about life, and now she was ready to live.

> ## My prayer for you:
> ❋   ❋   ❋
>
> COME TO ME, ALL YOU WHO ARE WEARY AND BURDENED, AND I WILL GIVE YOU REST. TAKE MY YOKE UPON YOU AND LEARN FROM ME, FOR I AM GENTLE AND HUMBLE IN HEART AND YOU WILL FIND REST FOR YOUR SOULS.
>
> DEAR HEAVENLY FATHER, I THANK YOU FOR THE CHALLENGES YOU BRING ME TO FACE EACH DAY. WITHOUT THESE CHALLENGES I WOULD NOT BE ABLE TO LEARN, TO GROW AND TO FULLY UNDERSTAND WHAT IT IS YOU HAVE IN STORE FOR ME TO DO WITH MY LIFE HERE ON EARTH. LIFE CAN BE HARD AND MANY TIMES CONFUSING, OFTEN PAINFUL AS WE SORT THROUGH EVENTS THAT HAPPEN TO US AND TO THOSE AROUND US.

I PRAY THAT YOU WILL PROVIDE ME YOUR SHOULDER TO LAY MY HEAD UPON, SO THAT I CAN RECEIVE REST AND BE REFUELED BY YOUR PEACE, LOVE AND UNDERSTANDING.

THESE THINGS I ASK IN YOUR NAME. AMEN.

CHAPTER THIRTEEN
Sincerity
❊   ❊   ❊

*"But just as you excel in everything—
in faith, in speech, in knowledge, in complete
earnestness and in your love for us—see that
you also excel in this grace of giving. I am
not commanding you, but I want to test
the sincerity of your love by comparing it
with the earnestness of others."*
2 Corinthians 8:7-8

Sincerity. The dictionary defines it as freedom from deceit, hypocrisy, or duplicity; probity in intention or in communicating; earnestness. Seems straightforward to me. But I guess even the simple things can become complicated.

My friends tell me they are going to shave their heads to support me. I've been bald for a while due to the chemotherapy that I'm taking to get rid of my cancer.

A lot of people think that you lose your hair because you have cancer. That's not true. Losing your hair is actually a side effect of the treatment that we take to get rid of the cancer cells. You see, our bodies are made up of 10 trillion cells. That's a lot of cells! Sometimes, these cells break the rules and decide to do whatever they want. They multiply and divide super quickly and start glomming onto each other to wreak havoc on our bodies. They are mean. And they have to be stopped.

One way to do this is to douse them with chemotherapy. Chemotherapy is a really strong medicine that can damage the cancer cells by annihilating them. (Yeah!) Unfortunately, chemotherapy is so strong that is also damages our normal, healthy cells (the ones who are following the rules). That is a bummer because our hair cells are part of the normal, healthy group.

So, when we take chemotherapy to get rid of the cancer cells, one of the side effects is that it also gets rid of the cells that make our hair grow, so we lose our hair. We even can lose the hair on our face and bodies, too.

That's a big deal! It's scary to lose your hair. It doesn't matter how old you are or if you are a girl or a boy. It is still scary. People stare as if I don't notice them staring at me. Sometimes, I just want to say out loud, "Yes, it's true! I have cancer!"

I shouldn't be ashamed of having cancer; after all, it's not my fault this happened to me. Despite me knowing this, ashamed is sometimes how I feel. So when my friends at school said they were going to

Chapter Thirteen: Sincerity

shave their heads to support me, this made me feel good. It made me feel like they cared.

My friends started a club and they were raising money for shaving their heads. They were donating the funds to childhood cancer research. One of our teachers was even helping us get matching t-shirts for the big event.

"It's now or never!" I said as we drove to the site where my friends were about to go bald. "Anyone going to back out?" I teased. "No way!" they chanted earnestly in unison. We pulled into our parking spot and walked proudly side by side, all of us wearing matching shirts and the girls wearing matching ponytails. Not for long...

We entered the venue and saw hundreds of people. The energy in the room was high. Music was playing and an emcee announced each group of people willing to be shaved. Some were on stage already in the process of being shaved. Others waited in the wings for their turn to be next. It was obvious who had already gone before us as their heads glistened under the lights, their hands repeatedly finding their way to their heads as if their hair would magically reappear.

We looked around for our teacher and didn't see her at first. We started talking to other friends and family members while we waited our turn. We had about 30 minutes until it was time.

Within seconds the mood changed. Our teacher approached with a nervous grin on her face. Not the kind of nervous grin where she was about to shave her head, rather a grin that looked like she was about to slap us with some bad news.

We circled around her as she started to speak. She was frantically telling us that the school's "competition" was in two days. All the girls with me that day were part of that, too. We all knew that. Why was she telling us this, and what did it have to do with our event today? As she continued talking she grew more uncomfortable. For crying out loud lady, you aren't making any sense! I thought to myself. She stuttered out the real reason she was there.

"Girls, I'm going to have to ask you not to shave your heads today. I need you to look your best for the competition. After that's over, we can all go down to the barber and shave our heads together! It'll be fun, O.K.?"

Did she just say what I think she just said? Um, hello! Bald kid standing right here! What did she mean by "look your best?" What is going on? We all stared at her with our mouths agape, shocked by her words.

Finally, one girl spoke and asked her why they couldn't shave their heads and also do the competition. What was the big deal? Our teacher explained that this competition was "really important" and that the girls needed to present themselves in the best possible light; being bald just wouldn't look "professional." Fumbling, as if to make herself feel better, she went on to explain that it was different for them as they were "choosing" to shave their heads, unlike me

Chapter Thirteen: Sincerity

who "had" to be bald because of the cancer. She asked them why a couple of days would matter.

I listened, stunned. It was as if she thought that losing my hair had made me lose all my feelings, too. At first, the girls protested, telling our teacher that they were going to shave their heads anyway and that they would explain to the judges at the competition why they were bald. They felt like the judges would understand and would think nothing of it. What they didn't realize was that they weren't going to be in the competition if they made the choice to shave that day.

It was a matter of minutes before all was understood. The clock was ticking down; our time to shave was quickly approaching. Pressure was building. What were they going to do?

Everyone turned and looked at me as if they needed my permission to walk away. What was I supposed to do? Their eyes were pleading with me and our teacher was nodding as if she were encouraging me to "do the right thing." What a disappointment she was. What kind of example was she setting, and what lesson was she trying to teach?

I shrugged and said to my friends, "Go ahead, you can do the competition and then you can shave your heads when you are done." They timidly asked, "Are you sure you don't mind?" I barely was able to nod my head.

The teacher breathed a sigh of relief and embraced the girls as if they were the heroes. Although they didn't seem pleased with their decision, they all gave me a hug and walked away. All of my friends walked, with the exception of one.

My most sincere friend stood by my side and said, "No, I'm not going!" The group came to a halt and looked at her with surprise. She went on to say things that warmed my heart. Things like, there is more to life than a school competition. That people are professional and beautiful because of what is inside their hearts, how they act and how they treat one another. They are not made less so by the mere fact of having or not having hair.

I stared at her, thinking she could easily have been on a stage reciting a beautiful Shakespearian soliloquy. I smiled as she spoke, her words filling my heart and soothing its most recent scars. She turned to me and wrapped her arms around me, hugging me closely with genuine love.

It's time. Let the shaving begin. As she climbed into the chair, she gave me a wink. Grabbing her ponytail, she handed it to the hairdresser, proclaiming, "Let's do this!"

My prayer for you:

❋ ❋ ❋

BUT JUST AS YOU EXCEL IN EVERYTHING—IN FAITH, IN SPEECH, IN KNOWLEDGE, IN COMPLETE EARNESTNESS AND IN YOUR LOVE FOR US—SEE THAT YOU ALSO EXCEL IN THIS GRACE OF GIVING. I AM NOT COMMANDING YOU, BUT I want to test the sincerity of your love by comparing it with the earnestness of others.

Thank you, God, for giving us the courage to stand up for what we know and believe is right.

I pray that You will fill me with the sense of right and wrong and nudge me frequently so that I can stand together with family, friends and strangers in order to do Your will. I also pray that my actions are filled with purpose and sincerity each and every day.

These things I ask in Your name. Amen.

CHAPTER FOURTEEN
Slow Motion
❊ ❊ ❊

"For I know the plans I have for you," declares the Lord, "plans to prosper you and not harm you, plans to give you hope and a future." Jeremiah 29:11

*B*efore, I could run.
Before, I could laugh without hurting.
Before, I could think quickly.
Before, I had a lot of friends.
Before, I was happy.
Now, everything has changed.

I used to be just a regular kid. I'd wake up, eat breakfast in my pajamas and then would get ready for school. After school, I played sports and did homework. I had friends over on the weekends and we'd play outside on nice days and watch movies inside when the weather was bad. I have a couple of siblings and let's be honest, sometimes I fought with them, but that's normal, right?

One day I am a "before," and the next, I am changed. Changed because of some cells gone mad. Where did they come from and why were they in my brain?

You'd think it would be easy. Cells gone mad form a tumor. The tumor causes me to suddenly do weird things. Things like shakily write my name, fall down, cross my eyes and get headaches.

The tumor is discovered.

People freak out.

Doctors reassure the ones freaking out that with a short course of treatment, all should be well within a year. That short course includes surgery, radiation and chemotherapy.

Doctors do their thing. I am changed.

Sure, I survived. I am alive and that tumor is gone, but what did it do to my brain? What did it do to me?

That tumor took hostages when it left my head hostages called speed, memory, balance, articulation and, worse, it took a little happiness, too. Sometimes, I don't even know who I am. I've been kidnapped and I can't find my way out to become who I once was, where I was safe.

It's a mind trip. I feel like I've been transported to a strange land where I'm standing in a circular room filled with doors. The doors are all sizes, and they beckon me to approach and turn their knobs. I'm scared standing there alone. I don't know what to do. I need to make a choice. Do I give up or do I fumble along in this fog?

Chapter Fourteen: Slow Motion

Somewhere far off, I can hear voices. They are encouraging voices. What is it they are saying? Maybe they want me to move, to open a door. Maybe I'll see their faces if I open a door. I inch slowly toward the closest one and turn the handle.

The door is heavy and hard to push. Finally, it moves. Creaking open, I see my past, and I see people and remember who they are. I remember those experiences and the emotions, too.

I blink and see faces staring down at me with looks that I can't understand.

Where am I? What has just happened? I recognize my family and start to tell them about these doors, yet the words don't come. Suddenly, I'm back in that strange land.

I start to cry. I don't even know why.

The doors are opening and closing in rapid succession. Numbers, colors, smells, sounds and words are all pouring from the rooms. Stop! Wait for me! I need to see what's there. None of this is making sense. I choose to push forward, hoping for some clarity soon.

I focus and there they are again. Family and the hospital staff surround me with commands.

"Can you lift your arm?"

"Can you say your name?"

"Do you know where your are?"

Finally, I can move a little. I slur my name and manage a strained smile. Everyone smiles back. Tears pour from my parents' eyes. They tell me they love me. What is happening?

I step into my new world of change.

My brain is a muscle that needs reconditioning. I'm ready now. I am no longer hostage. My body is weak, yet my will is strong.

I am part of a family who lives in faith. I look up to them because they encourage me to move forward no matter what life hands to us. They will be with me during my recovery and that gives me comfort. I want to get better for them. I want to get better for me. Mostly, I want to get better because I know, I can feel this deep inside, that I am going through this experience because God has a plan for my future. He has a plan for me to share my gifts with others. That gives me hope.

My plan included gifts that, at first, I didn't realize I had. I felt them, but didn't really know how I was using them. It took my parents, some friends and many adults telling me how I'm impacting others before I truly grasped what they were saying. To me, I just did what I knew in my heart was right to do.

Life is filled with choices. Every single thing we do is a choice. Along with our choices, we have outcomes. Those outcomes can be positive or more on the negative side. It all depends on what we decide.

There are some experiences that we as individuals don't choose to happen, like the cells in my brain going rogue. I didn't ask for this to happen. Who would? However, it is in situations like these when our choice in how we react comes into play.

Chapter Fourteen: Slow Motion

When I woke up from my surgery, I wasn't able to walk, talk or eat on my own. I felt like I was an infant inside a young person's body. That was not a good feeling, and I was ready to do whatever I needed to get back to my "old" self. That was a choice. I could have laid there and felt sorry for myself. But honestly, that hadn't even crossed my mind. I was ready to get moving! Where was my physical therapist?!

Walking was interesting. I was wobbly and even though my brain was telling my legs to move, sometimes they didn't move in the right direction. I had to have help in the beginning and needed a walker to keep me steady. Choices again. I could have just finished my physical therapy and said, "That was hard and I'm wiped out," and not tried to continue on my own. Or, I could choose what I did do, which was practice walking and set small goals for myself to achieve. With encouragement from my parents, the hospital staff and my friends (who includes my friend, Jesus), I did it!

Determination, fortitude, and diligence are all words that mean the same thing. In kid language, the meaning is simple: "Don't give up!"

What I realize is that if I continue to live my life making positive choices, picking how I respond to what is presented before me, I become a leader! I know I'm a kid, but kids can lead by example, too.

Most of the time, I don't understand how my choices impact those around me. I just do things with all my heart. I play sports, maybe a little differently, but I play with gusto. I go to school and work harder than I've ever had to work before, and I get really good grades. That makes me proud, especially since I've had to learn how to write with my opposite hand. I even play a musical instrument and use my wavering voice to recite lines in a play.

I hold my head high and embrace my new self. Joy exudes from my core.

Every now and then, I see a grown up wiping a tear from their eye and giving others in the room that "look." I think to myself, I'm just following what I hear in my heart from my trusted friend, Jesus. He is ultimately the one who I want to be the example for and He is the one who helps me every step of the way.

He is there for you, too. He is the best friend you'll ever know. Everyone wants that special friend in his or her life. He's already there inside your heart waiting; all you have to do is introduce yourself and your journey is ready to begin!

You don't have to be scared or feel awkward about talking to Him. Just be honest with Him, act like a kid with honesty and innocence and He'll give you all the support you need.

I used to think I was happy "before" and that I'd never be that happy again. It took a tumor in my brain for me to realize the true sense of the word.

Choice. It's powerful. It's life-altering. Make it God.

Chapter Fourteen: Slow Motion

My prayer for you:

❋ ❋ ❋

"FOR I KNOW THE PLANS I HAVE FOR YOU," DECLARES THE LORD, "PLANS TO PROSPER YOU AND NOT HARM YOU, PLANS TO GIVE YOU HOPE AND A FUTURE."

THANK YOU, LORD, FOR THE CHANGES YOU PRESENT TO ME EACH DAY. SOME ARE EASY TO HANDLE, WHILE OTHERS ARE HARD.

I ASK THAT YOU GUIDE ME THROUGH THE DIFFICULT CHANGES SO THAT I WILL BE ABLE TO CHOOSE THE MOST POSITIVE PATH TO FOLLOW. HELP ME TO USE MY CHALLENGES TO GUIDE OTHERS WHO ALSO STRUGGLE. IF WE ALL STAND TOGETHER IN OUR STRUGGLES, IT IS THEN THAT WE BECOME STRONGER.

THIS I PRAY IN YOUR NAME. AMEN.

Chapter Fifteen
Wailing Wall
❉ ❉ ❉

*"The desert and the parched land will be
glad; the wilderness will rejoice and blossom.
Like the crocus, it will burst into bloom;
it will rejoice greatly and shout for joy."*
Isaiah 35:1-2

My friend Woody Wolfe, Jr. started an incredible organization called Heart to Hands Ministry. The mission of his organization is to reach out through music, word and service, with the love, compassion and Good News of Jesus Christ to those who are in the midst of trial—especially for the families of children suffering from critical and chronic illnesses. Heart to Hands also hopes to encourage others to use their own unique, God-given gifts to reach out to a troubled, hurting world.

Front and center on his website is one of my favorite quotations, "Giving our Hearts to God and our Hands to Man." I love this statement! Woody gives his heart freely and touches lives all over our world. To know him is a gift; he's a rare treasure and is as humble as they come.

A Child Shall Lead

Woody spends most of his time inside children's hospitals bringing joy to kids and adults alike. He touches people's hearts and leads them to create positive change. He does this through his music, his words and his example. He also touches people through prayer.

Like Woody, there are hundreds of helpers in our world doing amazing things to better it. Spreading love, light and joy—but, sometimes, at a cost. Along with this joy, at times, comes pain. Emotional pain.

When you connect with people at deeper levels, you risk absorbing some of their emotions. Helplessness weighs heavily on our hearts as we listen to the words these kids share. While in our presence, the kids try to remain upbeat, but as they walk away, we see their shoulders slump as they again carry their own personal burdens, questions and fears.

We see their eyes searching in the distance for answers that may not be heard in words. We want to help, want to fix but are frozen in time, watching as our own hearts begin to crack open. We tuck our feelings back into these cracks and seal them up. This technique temporarily works, but soon the feelings will break through the seal, rushing out with built-up force.

We work in the busiest of places, full of noises, lights, rushing and crowds. If you take a moment to stop and actually see what's in front of you, coming on too fast, you will see the air thick with the emotions of others. We do our best to shield ourselves from the multitudes of pain before they get etched into our minds.

Chapter Fifteen: Wailing Wall

We see eyes that are listless, moist, wandering to a better time, a more beautiful place. People are lost, carrying bags with their necessities shoved inside. Coffee cups, snacks, magazines, sweatshirts, candy bars, but never a camera. This isn't a vacation—this is survival.

It's hard to understand why pain and hurt happen to people we care about. It seems overwhelming at times to try to figure it out. When I hear that my friends like Woody are asking for prayers for the kids and families in their hospitals, I happily oblige and lift them up in prayer as well. No heart is left unscathed when you work in a hospital filled with children. These kids have a passion for living, and that is what makes it so hard when they die.

Our grief can be an agent of change. Change can be positive or it can be negative.

If you suffer with complaint and anger then your experience will become negative. If you suffer with acceptance and grace, then you will be able to see how great this world is, and your pain will be lessened.

How do you suffer with acceptance and grace?

I see people walking around every day with profound emotional and spiritual wounds in their lives. They have deep scars, deep pain, yet they don't ask anyone for help. Maybe they find if they do, people will think they are weak or unable to carry out the tasks of their jobs. Maybe they feel like they don't have time to deal with these wounds. Just getting through the day can be difficult enough.

What I find interesting is that if these wounds were physical in nature, they would seek out medical attention immediately. We would see them in our emergency rooms frantic for help. Stiches, medication and advice would be administered to lessen their immediate pain. We are willing to go to a doctor, sometimes one we don't even know, for our physical pain, yet we don't accept help for our emotional pain.

The way to handle suffering, this emotional pain, with acceptance and grace, is through prayer. Before you roll your eyes, think about it for a minute. Prayer is everywhere. We have prayer warriors, prayer circles, prayer groups and prayer teams. People also pray independently of groups, praying in nature while hiking or biking. People pray in the solitude of their homes or in their cars as they wait at the light. Songs play on the radio that ignite a reason for prayer.

I do something called "drive-by prayers." When I'm walking around handling my day-to-day routine, I spot someone and call him or her up to prayer. Most of the time, I don't even know who they are or what hurts they have that may need healed, but I offer them up anyway. I ask God to sort that through for me, as He knows exactly what that person needs at that moment in time.

Prayer works. It does. Have you ever had a moment when a worry you carried just seemed to ease? Or have you ever had an idea that seemed to come out of nowhere that provided a solution to a long-standing question that no one knew but you? Someone's prayer fell to God's ears and He took that away for you. People are praying for you every day; you just might not know it.

There is enormous healing power in prayer, and I know a great doctor for you to see. His name is Jesus. Go ahead

Chapter Fifteen: Wailing Wall

and make an appointment with Him. I can vouch for His reputation. He is the best doctor around.

> **My prayer for you:**
>
> ❋   ❋   ❋
>
> THE DESERT AND THE PARCHED LAND WILL BE GLAD; THE WILDERNESS WILL REJOICE AND BLOSSOM. LIKE THE CROCUS, IT WILL BURST INTO BLOOM; IT WILL REJOICE GREATLY AND SHOUT FOR JOY.
>
> DEAR HEAVENLY FATHER, THANK YOU FOR GIVING US HEARTS THAT FEEL EMOTIONS SO DEEPLY. BECAUSE OF THIS WE KNOW WE ARE ALIVE! SOMETIMES, THESE FEELINGS ARE TOO INTENSE, TOO PAINFUL AND TOO MUCH TO BEAR. WHEN WE ABSORB THEM UNKNOWINGLY, WITHOUT UNDERSTANDING, WE BECOME VULNERABLE.
>
> I PRAY THAT YOU WILL WALK BESIDE ME, HELPING TO CARRY MY LOAD SO THAT ONLY LIGHT CAN ENTER MY SOUL. I PRAY FOR HEALING AND GROUNDING SO THAT I MAY CONTINUE TO DO YOUR WORKS.
>
> IN YOUR NAME I PRAY THESE THINGS FOR ALL OTHERS AND MYSELF. AMEN.

CHAPTER SIXTEEN
My Story
❊ ❊ ❊

"Blessed are the poor in spirit, for theirs is the kingdom of heaven. Blessed are those who mourn, for they will be comforted."
Matthew 5:3-4

It has taken me 20 years to share this, my own story. Before I could tell my story, I wanted to find answers to my questions. It's taken me this long to understand a funny thing: the answers were in front of me all along. I just didn't want to see them. I wanted the answers to be different than what they were.

It's not only taken me 20 years to understand the truth, but also to accept and embrace the truth. I've decided to share my personal experience with you because I want you to be able to embrace and find acceptance with whatever your personal struggle has been. I want you to experience inner peace by showing you ways to eliminate the negative perseveration that we tend to cling to in our lives.

I also feel it is important for me to share these words so that they might help someone else who is struggling with something similar.

From childhood, messages have been presented to me in my dreams. I get messages in other ways, too, but the ones that present themselves through my dreams are the strongest and most impactful.

About a year ago, I had the dream that would provide me the final explanation I needed, so that I could lay to rest my most burning question: "Why?"

This is how the dream transpired. I don't know where I was exactly, but I knew I was pregnant. I was shaking as I secretly took a pregnancy test. I stared at the stick, wanting so badly for it to show me the (+) sign. Looking at it, I saw a (+) sign, which means positive. To me, it also looked like a cross. A cross that was red in color.

Red is one of three primary colors and cannot be formulated by mixing any other color together. Being one of three is also symbolic of the Trinity; the Father, Son and Holy Spirit.

Red also has been associated with the color of blood, representative of Christ's death on the cross. In Christianity, Christ shed his blood while nailed to a cross, so that we could be saved, so that we could have salvation. His death atoned our sins.

His death, this *ultimate* sacrifice, provides a way for us to cleanse our souls and fill it with love, the joy of life, clarity and spiritual awakening.

The meaning of the word "cross" comes from the Latin word "crux," which means a guidepost giving directions at a place where one road becomes two. The cross is not just a Christian symbol. The cross also represents the four directions—North, South, East and West; four seasons—

Chapter Sixteen: My Story

Winter, Spring, Summer and Fall; or the four elements—Earth, Water, Air and Fire.

Ecstatic! I see clearly the red cross staring back at me. Having never had this feeling before, I finally was able to experience the emotion that everyone had told me about for years. Excitement filled my heart. I ran into the crowd to share with everyone my great news.

Suddenly, friends were surrounding me, showering me with attention, love, support and encouragement. I finally felt like I was accepted, like I belonged to this world, to the community of women.

I allowed myself to bask in this newfound feeling, letting go of the protective shield that I had so tightly clung to for years. It had been built to ward off the wounds that came with comments like, "It must be nice to just do whatever you want with your time," or, "I guess your career is more important to you than having kids," or, "Hurry up and have kids so our children can be friends," and, "Your life will never be complete until you become a mom."

In processing my new exciting information, instant realization sets in. I don't have a uterus. I quickly do a reality check to make sure my thoughts are processing correctly. Yes, the truth is, I don't have a uterus. It had to be removed early in my adult life due to years of suffering with debilitating and painful tumors, which caused a very poor quality of life.

Confused, I thought, *The pregnancy test said without a doubt that I was pregnant.* The symbol was clear and bold.

I thought, *Where will this baby grow? Can you be pregnant without a uterus?*

A Child Shall Lead

I began to panic and started to cry. Then I began to beg. I stood there and moaned, "Nooooo. Please, no." I rushed from friend to friend asking in desperation, "Can you be pregnant without a uterus?"

Their eyes were empty. They stood silent while shaking their heads. They began to fade away.

"Yes, you can!" I screamed. "Yes, you can! The baby could grow in my fallopian tube. Medicine can work miracles! This could happen!" My voice got louder, as if my desperation mixed with volume would change what is the truth.

My friends remained still, their faces telling me everything I didn't want to know.

I crumbled to the floor sobbing, choking on my breath as it got stuck in my chest. I screamed out, "Why? *Why??*"

Suddenly, I jerk awake lying in my bed.

Tears are streaking down my cheeks. My breath is rapid. My heart feels like it has literally been shattered into a million jagged pieces. I don't understand what is happening. Words, phrases and thoughts are quickly filling my head.

A few seconds go by and I realize there is a soft head lying on my shoulder. I have my arms around something warm, hugging it tightly. I wake up a little more to see my chocolate lab has managed to curl himself up into my arms as if he were hugging me, soothing away my pain.

He is an angel spirit. I know this to be true. He knows when my heart breaks without me saying a word. I gently kiss his head and let him know that I love him. I thank God for his presence and the comfort he provides to me while I again endure this familiar heartache.

Chapter Sixteen: My Story

This dream was an intense physical and emotional experience. I believe it was provided so that I could have an awakening. Through its power, I was given a source of healing, closure and acceptance.

This is what I have come to understand. The symbol of the cross and the color distinctly visible on that pregnancy stick relayed the symbolism of the struggle at a crossroads. There are many choices to be made in life, especially during times of trial.

The words that were flooding my brain as I woke up from this dream solidified my belief that God has created us specifically and uniquely with purpose. We are not an accident. There is not another human being who is exactly like me, and that is wonderful news!

Each of us is handed gifts, too—gifts that are meant to be shared and used for the good of the world. All of our gifts differ, and that is the point. We are designed to work in unison, bringing our varying gifts to the table in order to create the most powerful common good for the world.

Jesus also calls us out to be different. Because we are different, we will have different life experiences. Some will be easy and some will be hard. At times, we will experience sorrow in order to develop more deeply.

Sorrow isn't fun and certainly isn't easy to bear. We all carry sorrow in some way, again, differing in its cause. Instead of hiding this sadness, letting it hurt us, we need to share it with each other so that our sorrow can help someone else who may feel like they are all alone in theirs.

Broken hearts are real. They mean you are being touched by God in a special way. God can be found in "real" places,

places like hospital hallways, funerals, broken marriages, strained relationships, courtrooms and places where we work.

I believe that people with broken hearts understand "hope" in a deeper way. When hearts are broken, we come to understand things that there is no other way to understand. Sometimes, it takes this brokenness to push us forward in our growth so that we can ultimately achieve what it is that God has designed us to do.

It takes someone bigger and better than us to fix this brokenness. We think we can do it ourselves, but when we realize we are too broken and can't fix it ourselves, we need to call for help. This is not shameful or negative, to ask for help. This is the *only* way to heal.

This is why I am sharing my story today. I was stuck in my sorrow, and I was allowing that to cause negative energy to flow freely into my life. I was angry for a long time, questioning my purpose, my design. I stayed clear of women's groups as I let them make me feel like I wasn't "good enough" to belong.

For a time, I even stopped going to church, as I felt like I didn't belong there either. Our world likes to define for us what "family" is, and it took me a long while to understand that family doesn't look the same for everyone.

These negative feelings of anger, shame and disappointment stemmed from my deep sorrow and loss. In my grief I searched for answers, prayed and diligently tried to listen.

What I knew, though, even while believing myself to be disconnected from the "world," was that I never actually felt alone. All the while, God was there next to me, holding

Chapter Sixteen: My Story

me, reassuring me that I was special, that I was His and that I was loved.

The message of this dream goes beyond my own personal healing. That could have been provided in words, in pictures, symbols and sound. This particular dream created the strongest physical and emotional response I have ever experienced. It is because of this that I must share the most important part of the message.

We start with design, like the positive "cross" on the indicator of life. That hope brings excitement to people and a created future begins. This is a gift, something that should be treasured, as it is undeserved and unbelievable.

This gift is given in the purest form of love and light for the intention of sharing its goodness.

When these gifts (we as His children) are lost or broken, and we turn away from the one who provided it to us, God feels deep sorrow, as He knows we have made a choice that could ultimately harm us. It is when we are lost that our faith needs to kick in.

Through a sermon one Sunday, I heard a story that helped me visualize what faith really looks like. One night, a fire broke out in a neighborhood home. This house was two stories high and all of the bedrooms were located upstairs. There was a family of four inside, and the parents smelled the smoke and started to gather everyone up so that they could make their way to safety. The mom, dad and younger sibling made it out of the house, yet in the chaos of the moment, realized that their 9-year-old had been left inside. They were frantic, as the flames were too high and too hot to run back inside to get him. Panicking, they looked up at his bedroom window and saw that he had climbed out onto the window's ledge.

Screaming, the young boy shouted, "Daddy, Daddy, help me! Save me!" His father ran toward the house, shouting, "Jump, Son, I will catch you!" The little boy looked scared as the smoke and flames started to leap at him from behind.

Again, his father shouted, "Jump, Son, I'm here, I will catch you!" The little boy looked down, and all he could see was a cloud of smoke. He shouted back to his father, "But Daddy, I can't jump, I can't see you!" His father shouted back, "But I can see *you*...jump!"

Faith is the ability to take that leap, to jump regardless of what you are able to see.

I want you to understand, these words are not simple. Faith doesn't always come easy when loss and sorrow are involved. These words hold emotions that run deep and affect us to our core.

We feel this pain physically because we are tightly connected and intertwined with our Creator. This spiritual presence lives within us at all times, even behind the doors we may choose to close on Him.

When we feel empty, angry and alone, it is because we have closed the goodness off behind those doors. These doors need to stay open. Fresh air needs to circulate inside our souls.

Maybe it's too hard to open that door today. Maybe you start with just leaning on it from the other side. If you are too tired to open the door, rest against it and *He* will lighten your load. He is there.

Our God is ecstatic and hopeful for our futures. He created us uniquely and provides what we need to meet our

Chapter Sixteen: My Story

potential. He shares all of the emotions of an expectant parent and helps raise us along the way.

His arms are open. He will catch us. He is waiting with anticipation.

My prayer for you:

❋ ❋ ❋

BLESSED ARE THE POOR IN SPIRIT, FOR THEIRS IS THE KINGDOM OF HEAVEN. BLESSED ARE THOSE WHO MOURN, FOR THEY WILL BE COMFORTED.

WE ARE SO FORTUNATE TO HAVE A GOD WHO WILL PROTECT US, SURROUND US AND WALK WITH US EVERY SINGLE MOMENT OF OUR LIVES. I LOVE THE FACT THAT YOU HAVE TAKEN THE TIME TO DESIGN EACH OF US SO UNIQUELY AND PERFECTLY. I FEEL SPECIAL AND I THANK YOU FOR THAT, LORD! THERE ARE TIMES WHEN WE FORGET THIS GIFT.

I PRAY THAT DURING THESE TIMES, YOU WILL LEAD US TO THOSE DOORS THAT WE HAVE CLOSED OFF IN OUR HEARTS. PLACE OUR HAND ON THE KNOB SO THAT WE CAN OPEN THE DOOR TO YOU. HELP US TO SEE CLEARLY YOUR MESSAGE SO THAT WE CAN BE YOUR LIGHT IN THIS LIFE.

THESE THINGS I PRAY IN YOUR NAME. AMEN.

IN CLOSING
Discovery
❊   ❊   ❊

"May the God who gives endurance and encouragement give you a spirit of unity among yourselves as you follow Christ Jesus, so that with one heart and mouth you may glorify the God and Father of our Lord Jesus Christ. Accept one another, then, just as Christ accepted you, in order to bring praise to God." Romans 15:5-7

When I started the journey of writing this book, I wanted to accomplish several things. One, I wanted to be able to share stories of hope and inspiration as traveled through heartache. I wanted to be able to give value and meaning to the everyday person's experience so that their story would not be forgotten.

Secondly, I set out to write these stories in a way that both would shed light on the fact that God is ever-present in our lives and also that He wants us to have a relationship with Him. He loves us and walks beside us through every moment of life, whether we choose to recognize Him or not.

I also wanted to find a way to share the emotional influence that befalls to people who work alongside children, adolescents, young adults and their families who face medical and personal crises. There are thousands of helpers and healers in our world whose own hearts need tending. Life is a gift that, because of our brokenness, so often gets overlooked. I wanted to find a way to bring a little healing to those who are in need.

Lastly, I decided that I needed to step up and start practicing my own beliefs. I wanted a deeper relationship with Christ and I wanted to share my findings with others. Through the writing of this book, I wanted to be challenged to find what that meant for me. I dove into this with faith that the outcome would meet my goals. What I have found so far is that the process itself has been more rewarding than I could have imagined.

By looking back and talking to the people in these stories, my own walk with Christ became solidified. I found that God has a great sense of humor and will answer your questions, often in concrete ways. While a strong believer, I felt insecure about my knowledge of the Bible and how to use it to help others and myself. God presented to me each verse and instilled the messages firmly so that I could relay those through my writing. Because of this practice, I have become more comfortable sharing my experiences with others and I was able to let go of negative forces that I allowed to exist within me for so many years.

In Closing: Discovery

As I read and re-read my writing, the lessons of hope, joy, perseverance, judgment, kindness, acceptance and grace jumped out at me as a constant reminder that these messages are the ones intended for our unity as a people.

Isn't it wonderful that we get to live in a world that is so complex, so full of mystery and so diverse?

You have your own story. Think about it and play it out using a different lens. Everyone's journey is unique, yet somehow our paths intertwine. Remember who you are, who God intended you to be. Relish in your design! Use your gifts to help others and bring light and goodness to our world.

When you are faced with fear or pain, make a conscious choice to push through it with faith. Lean in, gain support from those around you, and spread your arms out wide. Most importantly, open your eyes and look up. May that *child* always lead you.

Acknowledgments

I started writing these stories down in a little spiral notebook many years ago. I carried this notebook with me on vacations, during my many moves and even in my "important belongings bag" that I grabbed while fleeing from a hurricane. I often wondered when I would finally sit down and start turning these stories into a formal book, yet knew that when the time was right, I'd feel it. This notebook was filled with lengthy notes, scribbles, tear stains, colored ink and ideas. The one thing it didn't include was a title.

With full gratitude, I give Colonel Jim Wilson, otherwise known as "Uncle Jimbo," credit for this amazingly sweet yet powerful title. He gave me this gift as we sat in a small, rural Mexican restaurant eating chips, salsa and tacos off of flimsy paper plates. Together, we sat in this out-of-the-way place debriefing about life and God's plan for each of us.

The Scripture titles that were chosen for each chapter came from my family and many friends, when asked to provide to me their favorite Bible quote and along with words describing what the verse meant to them personally. Thank you to Sharon Connolly, Patti Deppe, Kelli Gerwig, Kim Kuehnert, Colonel and Mrs. George Ojalehto, Mrs. Peggy Sheehan, and Colonel John A. Speicher for your incredible insights. As I used your quotations, I wove in part of your story so that you, too, would have a voice and could be a part of this collective work.

Thank you to Pastor Mark Traylor for encouraging me to put my own story down on paper and to the staff at Elevate Publishing for believing in my idea and encouraging me along the way.

To Darrin, for reading and re-reading each chapter often late at night. I am grateful for your honest and supportive feedback.

To the many people who were depicted in these stories, I thank you for allowing me the privilege to walk next to you during a vulnerable time.

To my #1 cheerleader Chrissy—my sister and best friend. Your unfaltering love and support of me is humbling. You are a treasure.

With immeasurable and unending appreciation I thank my mother (my momma), Anna, for her encouragement and inspiration. You lead by example with strength and perseverance. You have paved the way for us "Hart women" to become authors and I will always be in awe of your grace.

Most importantly, I thank God for the life He has given me and for the opportunities that He presents every day.

About the Author

A special education teacher and Hospital School program supervisor, Carla Anne Hart specializes in helping children with chronic illnesses and injuries. One of her passions is creating stories and resource materials to promote awareness and understanding. Hart lives in Boise, Idaho, where she enjoys spending time outdoors with her chocolate lab, Hershey.